TALES THROUGH TIME

Borgo Press Books by MICHAEL R. COLLINGS

All Calm, All Bright: Christmas Offerings
The Art and Craft of Poetry: Twenty Exercises Toward Mastery
Brian Aldiss
Dark Transformations: Deadly Visions of Change
The Films of Stephen King
GemLore: An Introduction to Precious and Semi-Precious Gemstones
The House Beyond the Hill: A Novel of Horror
In Endless Morn of Light: Moral Freedom in Milton's Universe
In the Void: Poems of Science Fiction, Myth and Fantasy, & Horror
The Many Facets of Stephen King
Matrix: Echoes of Growing Up West
Naked to the Sun: Dark Visions of Apocalypse
The Nephiad: An Epic Poem in XII Books
Piers Anthony
Scaring Us to Death: The Impact of Stephen King on Popular Culture
Singer of Lies: A Science Fantasy Novel
Tales Through Time: Selected Poems, Revised and Enlarged Edition
Three Tales of Omne: A Companion to Wordsmith
Toward Other Worlds: Perspectives on John Milton, C. S. Lewis, Stephen King, Orson Scott Card, and Others
Wer *Means* Man, *and Other Tales of Wonder and Terror*
Wordsmith, Part One: The Veil of Heaven: A Science Fantasy Novel
Wordsmith, Part Two: The Thousand Eyes of Flame: A Science Fantasy Novel

TALES THROUGH TIME

SELECTED POEMS

REVISED AND ENLARGED EDITION

by

Michael R. Collings

Emeritus Professor of English
Seaver College
Pepperdine University

THE BORGO PRESS

MMX

Borgo Laureate Series
ISSN 0182-3336

Number Seven

Copyright © 2010 by Michael R. Collings

All rights reserved.
No part of this book may be reproduced in any form
without the expressed written consent
of the author and publisher.
Printed in the United States of America.

www.wildsidebooks.com

FIRST EDITION

CONTENTS

Part One: On the Morning of Christ's Nativity 7

Part Two: Still Secrecies of Love—Poems LDS and Other 17

Part Three: Abraham's Confession of Faith 127

Part Four: My Witness and My Truth: The Testimony of Alma .. 143

Part Five: Pinnacles of Stone—Reflections of an Aztec World .. 173

Index of Titles 208

About the Author 211

PART ONE

ON THE MORNING OF CHRIST'S NATIVITY

On the Morning of Christ's Nativity

In December of 1629, the twenty-one-year-old John Milton composed one of his first great works, his Nativity Ode. Using the trope of writing the poem at the first light of day on Christmas morning, in fact looking out his window to witness the arrival of the three orient Kings, he presents himself as hastening to compose a "humble ode" to lay at the feet of the Christ Child. What follows is an entirely non-traditional Christmas poem, one that ranges from the infant Christ asleep in the manger to the image of the pagan gods trooping in defeat into Hell at the mere coming of the Child. In twenty-seven meticulously structured and rhymed stanzas, the youthful poet (whose adult works would include what is arguably the greatest single poem in the English language, *Paradise Lost*) explores the global and cosmic ramifications of the Incarnation in tones that move magnificently and seamlessly from the intensely personal to the unlimited universal. For any poet, the poem would be a masterpiece; for a poet of twenty-one, who had yet to publish a single poem, it is nothing less than miraculous.

The following piece, strictly modeled on Milton's stanzaic form and rhyming pattern, and borrowing (in a perfectly acceptable seventeenth-century manner) his title, represents my own attempt at expressing the roles and functions of the Infant Christ. It represents at once a statement of my deep appreciation of Milton and his works, gleaned from over forty years of engagement with them on various levels, and—more crucially—a personal vision of Christ as both God and Man. It would be ingenuous to argue that it should not be compared with Milton's achievement; but at the least I hope it does not fare too poorly in the comparison.

THE ODE

It's dark and drear today,
The sky a numbing gray,
    With cloud-banks bowing near to brush the ground;
The wan white snow is gone,
Absorbed into the lawn
    That stretches in brown desolation 'round,
While in the barren garden beds
The first brave tulips break, to raise their gladsome heads.

    II
And in my heart I yearn
For Spring's rainbowed return,
    And wish that I were now in Other-When;
That darkness veiled the land
And in a starry Band
    Bright Angel courses, far as eye could ken,
Proclaim in verses pure, and call
The advent of Good Will and Peace on Earth to All.

    III
If I were Other-Where
And heard that holy Air
    Resounding over shepherds' eager ears,
Then might I join the throng
And know that I belong
    With hosts of worshippers who shed all fears,
Might joyfully meld my song with them
And journey through dark vales to distant Bethlehem;

IV

Where Mary enfolds her Son,
Her strenuous labors done,
    Near Joseph, steward of the mortal Maker
Chosen from before
Wild oceans voiced their roar
    Or whispered in a world-wide, blue-froth breaker;
Or eagles soared through tumbled skies,
Or spirit shone through lion's, tiger's, lynx's eyes.

V

Elected ere each world
In cosmic order whirled
    About a thousand thousand thousand stars;
A simple child, to grow
And know both joy and woe
    That mark His trail of days like shadow bars;
Though Son withal of Father-God,
Content to bear His pall of needful flesh-façade.

VI

In that Other-Where
A rough-hewn manger, bare
    Of all but fragrant golden straw,
Would serve as cynosure
Within the night obscure,
    And silent eyes—now moist with tearstains—draw
From Heaven to long-expectant Earth
As simple shepherds greet an Infant's Holy Birth.

VII

The Child with eyes tight-closed,
His fragileness exposed
    To all the vagaries of mortal life,
Sleeps peacefully and dreams
Perhaps—or so it seems—
    Of Heaven's rest exchanged for earth-bound strife,
Of praises formed on every tongue,

And crystal anthems by hosts of Angels freely sung.

VIII

Or should we still extend
Beginnings without End
3   And see Him in divinest Councils speaking;
Where two exalting Plans
Are offered forth, for Man's
    Eternal Destiny and Fate both seeking;
Intelligences without start,
As Spirits clothed, hear that each must soon depart;

IX

And whether yet impelled,
By One's strong will compelled
    To troop in irons back to Heaven's cell;
Or if by faith return
And endless honors earn,
    Or fail, and through their choices merit Hell—
The lot is theirs—no vote constrained;
Each heart is free, and thus, strict agency maintained.

X

Some seek the safest way,
That in stolen freedom lay,
    Where One will force each Spirit's right decision,
And joined in gleeful mirth
At those whose trial on Earth
    Might end with them soul-bound by Sin's derision,
While they who chose in fear this plan
Were guaranteed safe-conduct back to God, as man.

XI

But more were stirred by Him
Whose Plan at first seemed grim,
    Since it retained the chance that some might fail;
But those whose true Will spoke
Would break Perdition's yoke,

And after trials endured in bodies frail
Might through the Son's unending Light
Thus prove themselves full worth Celestial Worlds bright;

XII

And sing forevermore
Creation's mighty score
    From worlds unnumbered through perpetual Space,
And hymn with one accord
The Glories of their Lord,
    Whose life and death rang greatness for their race;
While every note to Him thus sung
Trebles but the praise of God from every tongue.

XIII

But would that be too much
Encumbrance laid on such
    A sweet and tender Babe as this here sleeping?
Would the jading weight
Of untold worlds' fate
    Disturb his pleasant rest with weary weeping?
Is this too great a burden still
For One so tiny, weak, and helpless to fulfill?

XIV

If aye, then we must turn
To future years to learn
    How His Plan's fruition might unfold;
But oh! that leads to fears
And terrifying tears
    Upon a high and lonely Mountain cold,
Where He alone must suffer woe,
And He, of all God's Sons, alone to Death must go;

XV

And so conclude His Word
By countless Spirits heard
    That He thus takes upon Him Mankind's sins,
And by that selfless Act
Completes the Eternal Pact,
    And Heaven's approbation fully wins;
While millions taste their pented breath—
In awe, regard on High the instant of His Death.

XVI

To tarry at that sight,
Or marvel at His plight,
    Would prove too much for mortal heart to bear;
To look beyond were wise,
A respite for frail eyes
    And solace to all hearts worn thin with care;
For through His death he works a change
And fashions thus a vessel for our souls' exchange.

XVII

For after three dark days
He our full forfeit pays,
    With broken heart and blood for Mankind shed;
And with the morning dew
Arises—Lives!—anew
    And walks this Earth with simple footsteps' tread;
'Mid lilies white and diamond pure
He works for us forever deadly Sin's last cure.

XVIII

But now the Infant sleeps,
While Mary softly weeps
    In joy and sorrow for the coming years;
And falters, filled with awe!
At Mercy wedding Law
    And treasures up great promise mixed with fears;

And in His face, composed and fine,
She sees the coming Judgment of great Adam's line.

XIX
For the bright Son dawns with Power,
Whose Might and Grandeur flower
    With full achievement of His chosen Task,
And mounts above wide throngs
Repentant of their wrongs,
    Content in His great Presence now to bask;
While he with Wisdom's somber grace
Consigns each spirit to its well-appointed Place;

XX
Until each Heavenly Sphere
Bides, eager to draw near
    The seat of Radiance and ethereal Throne;
Across the cosmic waste
Each planet waits in place
    To feel the sear of flame that each must own
Before they wheel through reverend skies
And humbly bow before their loving Sovereign's eyes.

XXI
And He will judge each kind,
Each Making of His Mind
    On counted Worlds that whirl without End;
From them accept His Crown
Of Honor and Renown,
    And every knee in every Where shall bend
In recognition of His power
Foretold, and now encompassed by this final hour.

XXII
Then the Creator-Son
His mortal conflict done,
    Will fold all Cosmos in His firm embrace,
Where vast Intelligence

Uncounted Eons hence
    Will praise His Name and magnify His grace;
And each, enrobed in flesh and bone
Renew the Plan and seek progression as His own

XXIII

But no! it is not so;
For us there can be no
    Other-Where or Other-When than here;
Let us softly leave
While day-larks gently weave
    Their lullabies to fall on Infant ear;
And let Him, as we found Him, sleep
Surrounded by poor shepherds, with their lowly sheep.

XXIV

The sullen clouds have fled,
By day's sweet brightness led;
    And in my heart I find a welcomed bliss;
For while the Infant dreams,
The nooning Sun now beams
    And on my burgeoning garden leans to kiss
The warming earth and interpose
With crowning Iris spears, the Lily, and the Rose.

PART TWO

STILL SECRECIES OF LOVE

POEMS LDS AND OTHER

The poetry in this collection represents most of my published L.D.S.-oriented poetry, or poetry published in primarily L.D.S. journals and magazines, over the past forty years. Many have been revised although few have been so heavily altered as to disguise their earliest form or content; many have subsequently been revised for form and content and appear thus altered in other collections. Some began as hurried notes scribbled at odd moments during my two years of service in the Germany North Mission; others reflect specific insights during my graduate studies in Milton and Renaissance Literature; still others reflect particular events that have altered my life in large and small ways. All depend upon my ideas and beliefs and should be understood as poetry rather than as doctrine or history.

INTIMATIONS
"Trailing clouds of glory do we come...."
—William Wordsworth

When we left God's presence, did we stand,
Childlike at the gates, eyes downcast,
As in stark fear or trepidation, and
Contemplate with grave observance our last
Sweet moments of security before the grand
Release, before wan infant wings flurried souls
Into their unknown worlds, their worlds of flesh,
Of sorrow, pain, of brightly ceaseless goals
That withdraw with every footstep nearer, fresh
Trials to toss us as refuse on oak-stern boles;
Or did we know, pellucid in pure power,
The strength we bore within to stand against
Dark moments, search throughout obscurant hours
To touch with fragile hope that Love once sensed
While, childlike at the gates, we blessed our natal bowers?

For an Infant

A chosen sprit
hovers eagerly,
casts earnest eyes
around GodFather's world
to reassure,
imprint
all that was
and is yet to be.

The spirit
breathes...once,
twice,
a final time
draws in celestial fire,

Descends
through spheres of air,
through waters gathered beyond the heavens,
descends as if on feather-down
to sweetly solid earth,

To become…
A Child.

BEARING TESTIMONY

Carrying it with words
Slowly through life-jungles
To place it
In its litter
On the altar—
Sacrifice for all

CELESTIAL

Beyond WhitehotWhite…White-beyond
    LightBrightWhite to
Embrace allColor/noColor in[-]
    Finite whorls

Image beyond Imaginations,
    World beyond AllWorlds,
Idea transcend-/transform-ing in[-]
    To God-Breath life

CenterSoul of Joy (Cause and
    End of human life),
Place of Peace, Universe-sheltered
    Images of Love

Silence in sound; whispering
    Sound of heartbeats
tandembeating [in-]to Unity—
    Vision—Being—Awe—

ThricegreatCreation's triple
    Harmonies enscale One
Grand symbolic
    All…

And beyond—
    Celestial words form
WorldsCelestial, SoulsCelestial…form
    MortalGods

TERRESTRIAL

Earthlike — solid — heavy with the weight of
Iron, stone. Bristlecones three thousand ages
Old — Redwoods ringing human lives above
Minuscule tufts of crocheted fern. Pages
Grow and shift and turn and die. Weight endures.
Earthlike — solid — heavy with time and life
And immortality. Soft polished curls
Of evanescent violets scent white-
Grey-green rosettes of thistles leaves beneath
Thick, bristling cups that spill purple freight in
Waiting air. Broad roadsides, thin winding paths,
Faint trails to beauties baked in summer's sun ...

All heavy — Earthlike — weighted weighted with
Pervasive Life — God's solemn second Gift.

TELESTIAL

Distant, star-like, farseeing—far
        from bright vividness of God. Fires

of Creation mate with tired embers,
        grey-flames half-remembering

Glories of another, further Sphere;
        but still—distant, farseeing—even there

Harmonies exceed all that we know
        upon this fragile globe,

all that we faintly understand
        and struggle to apprehend.

From a distance, farseeing, grey-
        based worlds blend brick with rays

of greening life. Promise flecks
        brazen starlight, distant, farseeing, back-

ward-seeing through Infinities to look
        upon the Throne it once could

comprehend, no more. At the last,
        it accepts third, not second, best.

CREATION: *DE MATERIA*

Free elements, unwilled, thrice uncontrolled,
Coeternal with first Absolutes
Though formless in Infinity—
    Formless left
             Until beginning
                    chronic
            throbs of Time;

Free elements
Beyond hegemony of motile Gods
To be created or destroyed,
    Self-existing, self-determining,
        With full volition
Whirl and mist in fiery dance at prime Commands,
Conjoin and fuse into all mortal globes,
    Unnumbered worlds
            Worlds numbered only to
Presiding Councils of High Gods.

And from warm dust,
                            fresh living dust,
            Matter fully agent for its destiny,
The Highest Councils formed,
In-formed with agency inherently supreme
A mask with which to hull immortal fire.
Thus man became a living soul,
God-potential in his will.

A Christic Century
29 October 1972
Poem 100
In the Manner of George Herbert

These syllables proclaim my deep-wrought *thoughts*
In *lines* and numbers that denote *my* hope
Of Life *and* strength, power of *heart* through Him.
Through twenty *years* and five *my* life has run,
And if few rhymes *are soul* inspired, still
Remains the hope *my given* gift be tuned
To sing His *rule* of love *o'er* erring men.
And we *shall* know in Him the path *to* joy;
Our *love* reflects the image of *His* care,
His loving care for all — Come, join my *praise.*

THE STAR-FILLED CANOPY
For Judith Reeve

"...überm Sternenzelt muß ein lieber Vater wohnen."
—Beethoven

Low in the West above sharp spear-thrust pines,
Hesperus, bright Venus, scintillates,
Her clear soprano mingling with broad bass
Of Earth's dark ponderous song in sweet duet;

Till gradually all-shimmering choirs of Stars
Appear and wheel along arched velvet courses
In concert, deafening the listening night
With one great voiceless, full-voiced Harmony.

"Above the star-filled canopy
must a loving Father dwell."

NOVA

Once
a man glowed
like a class-G star
moderately, and lit a world.
A man born of woman (as the saying goes)
of flesh and blood, neither wholly saint
(at first) nor wholly sinner (and at
the last, no sinner at all).
In fine, a man,
once.

But
the man (as
science says the stars
might someday do) gathered in
his essence, concentrated his brilliance
until flesh and blood shattered into
immortality — a million times a
million times his brightness
when he was only
a man;
but

there
analogy
fails. For a sun,
if it should nova, would surfeit on its
elemental fuels in final radiance and consume its
progeny (Saturn-like consuming Saturn) and itself as well
and then pull in upon its husk a mask of darkness
to huddle in a blackened corridor
of space, distorting light

and gravity
there.

But

the man,
the human-nova who now
is God, expanding, thus will burn
more brightly with each breath of praise
until no mortal darkness can survive at all
and even Sol's fine ash will shine as molten silver
in His light. And Man of Holiness, a million
times a million times as He is now,
will continue without end
of Time: the man,
the human-nova,
God.

TO BECOME A CHRIST
for Orson Scott Card,
who *felt* the way

*

Invisible man launches himself in null-g —
Sacrificial Lamb

**

His sacrifice sliced flesh to flesh
Harvested flesh from flesh

Unwept tears bore acid furrows in a soul
Roiled with lost souls

They shed tears of pain and fear, and cursed his steps
Spat blood beneath his steps.

Fear and hate and love compounded in
Single continuous desperate act

Love defined the sacrifice: Their pain for life —
His pain for truer, greater life

***

Music cuts severs heart from mind and hand —
 in exchange a residue of glory, and a song.

****

On a distant world a sparrow falls with
none to mourn and none to

see. He kneels, stigmata palms pressing into bent
knees, beneath a darkness Rood-shadow

thin. And weeps. A knife glints — his feet
twist beneath his weight and ghost

pain along his arms. Temples throb. Flesh pours agony

like heated wine. And yet.... And

yet the point drops pierces penetrates
And spills new blood upon *this*

earth. On a distant world a knife descends. A Christ
Completes his deadly sacrifice.

* * * * *

Is it enough to think the pain? To speak the
Sacrifice?

Does it benefit the more to *feel* the slice of
Shepherd's blade?

The nothingness of severed hands below urgent
music never born?

Should I link to *raman* suffering and share
it through the mind?

Or be just *be* a pain-drawn Christ praying
Beneath a Tree of Sacrifice.

CHRIST OF UNIVERSE

Christ of Universe, eight-finger-splayed
resemblance of heshe's stern Quadrinity,
stood comfort on a hillock just beyond

the swell of pallid blades. Corved of liquid
aurum in a stasis-field, it towered
over heshes' node. Waters met there.

Heshe chose the place of waters for their
node, accreting with each generation
body-lozenge-fundament for heshe spawn.

Each Bright, smooth bearers took the path to Christ
of Universe and laid at ParentChildBodySoul
their offerings, while sowers toiled among

the stalks. Each Dark, sowers retraced the way
and bowed in darkness to Christ of Universe
and lipped the SingSong of Quadrinity,

ParentChildBodySoul. Bearers burrowed
heshe young while sowers bowed.
Later, beneath the ever-solid black of night

when glolights died...when heshe bearers
opened hirmselfs to living seed......when heshe
sowers sought other fertile fields...

they could not see, but knew beyond the hillock,
Christ of Universe stood comfort over heshe,
eyestalks poised, eight-finger splayed.

TO THINK

"Amazing what such a small thing can do,"
He said after they left…slunk away
Actually, to find some secret few
Moments together before new day
And consequences dawned.
       He tossed it,
Feeling heft and weight, its moist flesh cool
In his bare palm.
      "Amazing," and bit
Into the broken skin, its slick jewel-
Ruby strong against the white-sweet meat.
"To think that they would make a blunder
This immense…."
       It dropped to his still feet
As distantly, he felt the roll of thunder….

The Foundations of the Worlds

> For the worlds which He has saved are organized upon the principles of obedience and sacrifice; obedience, that all creations might thereby come to know themselves; and sacrifice, that all might render their Selves again to God.

I.

Isaac, my son, sole child of my waning years,
Fulfillment of the promises of God!
Isaac, no more a child but now a youth
About to step into the world of men.
Surely you must wonder at the strangeness
Of this our journey, near unto the Mountain
In the land of Moriah,
To offer sacrifice unto our God, Jehovah,
To Him who led me from the pagan lands
Toward this home
And promised me Posterity through you.

Do you not wonder
At your unaccustomed load—
Branches for the sacrificial fire?
At the lack of ram for offering?
Isaac, my son,
And Sarah's only child,
Do you feel it?
Do you know?

Deep within lost memories,
I seem to see great lithic gods

My fathers worshipped,
Gods of silent Stone,
Whose sole appeasement lay
    In infant flesh,
        In dying youths,
            In slaughtered maidens;
And I then questioned
How a god that fed on death
Could ever be a force
    Of life
        And of creation.
I rebelled. I flung them down,
Shattering them into small fragments—
Tokens of my disbelief.
For that great crime was I exiled
    From my land,
        From my city,
           From my home;
To search for Him,
The Creator, not created images.
And now ....

I have served Him all my days,
And in the twilight of my evening
He requires upon this stone
The innocent blood of dawning youth.
Was it for this that I fled Ur
And its false gods?
To sacrifice my son,
To touch my knife to his young flesh
As the priests of Ur
Sought to slay me years ago?
Isaac, my son!
Jehovah gave your soul to me
To guide and teach;
If He require you back again
By my hand slain,
So shall it be!

My Son!

The lives of those who serve our God
Are never easy.
      Blesséd, yes;
                But never easy.
In the century through which my life
Has run, how often,
Yea, how often has He demanded all?
Exiled from Ur, my home,
To wander in dry desert paths,
Losing to death's heavy pall
A father, weak but loving;
Twice—
      Once in Egypt's fertile plain,
      And once again
                In King Abimelech's court afar—
Nearly losing life and loving spouse,
Sarah, Princess of the Lord;
Often in our desert travels
Losing flocks and herds,
To have the Lord repay.
But now He asks that I relinquish
That which I can never find again;
You, my son—
      And with you,
             That Posterity
By which the Lord
Should spread His Name abroad
Throughout the land.
It is you, my son,
That I now leave behind,
As I have treasures left
Throughout my life;
Trusting in His wisdom and His love
That what I do is that which He desires
To bring about some greater joy.

My son, watch carefully the birds
High in the hidden blue;
Breathe deeply honey-laden air;
For you will have no chance again
To see the splendors of this earth.
      Another future,
             More glorious far
Than anything your father here
Could offer you
Awaits.
The Lord commands
And I obey.
    Do you feel it?
         Do you know?

II.

I know,
    But must not speak of what I know
        To him.
Father looks so old
Because he too knows;
It is no usual sacrifice
That Abraham must offer up today.
In a dream last night,
A Voice awakened me,
Told me of events to come,
Opened to my mind
    The role
        That I shall play
In my father's greatest trial.
A Voice of comfort;
And now I know that I am to die
        Today,
Upon Jehovah's cold-slab altar-stone.
I suppose that I should fear,
    Or weep,
    Or gnash my teeth in anger,

                    In defiance
Against God, Heaven, and great Abraham;
But how can I,
A youth whose every moment's wish
Has been fulfilled,
Whose life has been of joy
And richest blessings from his Lord?
If my father's God
And mine,
The Living God who led him out of Ur,
         Require my death in sacrifice,
                    I am prepared.

It pains me so to see
My father's sufferings,
But he must make his choice
                    Alone,
Without the knowledge
That I, too, have passed this test,
Have found the strength
To submit myself to God's commands.
Father, do not sorrow!
The teachings of your life
Support me in this hour.
Ahead, I see the mount,
       The stone that shall,
                 In my last moments,
Be my bed and hold my body
While my spirit rises up to Him above.
Father, do not sorrow;
       My Lord,
                 I am ready.
                        Take me.
I come to Him whose child I am.

III.

Abraham.

Abraham!
     Stay thy weaponed arm.
          Slay not thy bound and helpless son.
The Lord, thy God, hath tested thee
And found thee perfect in obedience.
Know now, thou son of man,
The sacrifice of this,
    Thy son,
        The promised child,
           Through whom thy name
And thy Creator's Name
    Shall be spread forth
        Through all the earth,
Was in similitude
    Of the greater Sacrifice
        That is to come,
When He who is to come
    Will lay down His own life
        Upon an altar made by men—
An altar cruciform,
Raised upon a mount of death—
And God, the Father of all life,
Will with full love
Assent that men might slay
His only Son.

Thou, Abraham, hast proven thyself.
Thy obedience in intent
Requires not
The culmination of this sacrifice.
Indeed, behold, within the thickets
Hath thy God a ram prepared,
    Pure and spotless
        For the Sacrifice.
Release thy son,
    Return unto thy home,
        And live with God's unending love.
Abraham,

> Farewell.

IV.

They're late!
It should not take this long
For them to offer up the sacrifice....
How proud my Abraham must be
To have our son accompany him
Up to the Mount of Sacrifice.
He's a fine boy,
> Isaac.
I miss him so,
Even when he's gone but these few hours.
And Abraham, my companion
> Through the years—
>> Through our trials and blessings
>> From the Lord,
>> Through wandering childlessness—
And now we have a son.

Abraham seemed worried as they left,
Early, before the rising of the sun.
He often shares his cares with me,
But this time ....
I could feel deep tension in his voice,
His eyes,
As he looked at me
And at our son!
Then suddenly a feeling struck—
> So foolish—
That I would see my son no more!
What could happen to the boy
Upon known paths,
> Protected by his father
>> And by the Promises of God?
That foolishness is past;
My son is well.

He will grow to be a man,
    A man of sacrifice,
        A man of God,
To whom the things of God alone
Are worth.
Abraham has taught him well
That man must first obey the laws
Of God
Before all hopes of earth and flesh.
Even if his body die,
My son shall live with God in spirit.
What should I fear of death:
    Abraham's,
        Isaac's,
           Or my own.
Death,
Which merely brings us back
To God,
    To home.

The sun is setting now;
They should be coming soon.
Yes, there they are ....
Father,
Son,
Silhouettes against an opal sky.
And all my foolish wondering
In vain.
    They both return;
        Abraham,

                                    Isaac.
All is well.
          All is well.

SEEDS

Thoughts,
      Feelings,
           Impressions,
Swell within,

Awaiting only that certain season
      To germinate,
           Push through rich loam
Into the open air of consciousness,

And bloom,
      Reflecting resplendently all beauties
           Of Him
Who sowed the seeds.

HANDS
For President and Sister Rees, Germany North Mission

A statue in a village square,
Christ, our Shepherd,
Standing there
With hands and arms outstretched,
Inviting all to share
Celestial love
And patient Master's care:
    Underneath, the message fair:
    "Come unto me."

Then war ... the searing of man's hate
And greed exchanging for the sacred scene
Destruction desolate.
The Christ-creator
Now a rubble unCreate;
His offer spurned by human wolves
Who would His Godhead desecrate:
    The world had closed the one true Gate:
    "Come unto me."

A statue in a village square;
A Christ, rebuilt from fragments
Sought for, found, rejoined with care
By repentant, loving hearts.
The ancient statue, in silence there;
But with no hands—of them no trace.
It stands, a message for all hearts to share:
    Underneath, in letters fair:
    "Christ has no hands but ours."

AN ACT OF LOVE

Christ's hands
and feet
hang pierced
for us;

He thirsts,
sorrows,
succumbs
in pain.

We slay
anew
Him with
our sins;

And with
our tears
Him free
again.

SACRAMENTAL SONG

White tray of Flesh — white tray of Blood —
Mortal Manifest —
Water clear and parted Bread —
Symbols — earthly dressed —

Touch our Lips to Charity —
Touch our Tongues to Truth —
Taste — with Organs never born —
Still Secrecies of Love —

White trays pass on — clear water dims —
Bread sleeps — only bread —
Wake anew — in Child-hood —
This Congregation — fit —

DURING SACRAMENT

The newest Deacons stand shoulder-tall to almost-
Teachers, buckle-tall to towering
Priests behind the white-clothed table; they fall
in serried ranks until empowering
words release them, both new and almost-Teachers—
white-shirted, tied. At the back, on folding
seats, three Teachers sit abreast, young features
solemn as they watch younger brothers hold
and pass the Emblems prepared for others
in their faith to eat and drink. Between,
long pews murmur movement as fathers, mothers,
children—each with sacred, intent mien—
join in community, and in concord
consecrate one heart to His soundless Word.

*KEU

Swelling, as a nine-month's child
That kicks and roils within the womb
And struggles to burst its membranous sphere
And succeeds — a new Life to make mine complete.

Swelling, as a new-sown seed
Startled by showers and wrapped in warmth
And wrenched within — first stirrings of leaves —
To burst ... an oak, a grapevine, a rose.

Swelling, in full-bloom power,
The word expands from mouths ages dead:
Keu, powerful, masterful — growing to
Kurios ... Kurikon ... Lord!

> [*Keu,* Indo-European root, meaning 'swelling', 'powerful' — developed into Greek *kurios*, 'lord,' and provided the root for *Church*, literally 'House of the Lord']

PATIOR: THE PULSE OF PAIN

Cruciform —
Blood blooms, nails bloom
Silver petals — huddling
In caverns of claw-curled palms
Shadowing

Blood drops
To soil — curves a hillock
Thigh — curls in dying dust —
A map, a markery of life
Unmarked

The cup
Crusted gold of clotted blood —
Hangs upon the memory — chased
Raised rime of rueful garlanding,
It will not pass.

Arms arch
Swan-arch embracing pain —
Back bow-burdened lungward
Lunging through
Darkness

Death holds
His breath — and will not
Strike. Bruised nerves taut taunt
Tissues torn and dipped like sops
In bursting blood

That pounds

And groans through bursting heart ....
And dark and calm and silence
Stillness, chill
Of death.

But all of this is futile sound,
Words that cannot broach the pain
Which we — if we are one with Him —
Shall never know
nor ever need to feel.

JOSEPH

Fountain clear of living water,
Oracle more fine and pure
Than any graced by green-wood goddess,
Guarded by swart, vengeful gods of old.
The fount, from which pours forth
In rich profusion,
Truth,
The Word of God restored.
Then Carthage ....
      And a parching thirst.

A light ordained to blaze the way
To God, to that one path
By mankind long obscured.
A lesser light—
Not He, the Source
Of all Eternal Light and Truth;
But rather he, the messenger,
The Chosen of the Lord.
Then Carthage....
      And a darkness palpable.

A field of knowledge, nurtured,
Tended by the same who husbands all.
A field not fully ripe for harvest,
Fruits of mind and spirit yet
To pluck,
To taste,
And be by all enjoyed.
But vandals ...
Wantons.

Then Carthage ....
    And consuming dearth.

A breath of life, warm and soothing,
Bringing wisdom, comfort, warning;
Yet like a mighty, raging storm:
"Thus saith the Lord!"
For while in flesh he saw his God,
Heard the Voice,
Received the Call,
A Prophet for all time.
Then Carthage ....
    And silence.

    Fountain quenched,
    Light obscured,
    Barren earth,
    Ungodly, deathly still.
    Carthage....
        And the end.

The End! no, rather a Beginning,
As Phoenix-like, Eternal Truth
Arose, and from the smoldering ruin,
His earthly pyre, took wing
And spread, as if a mighty wave,
The world o'er.
Elemental Truth,
Revealed by God,
Restored, confirmed, and testified
By Prophet's life
And blood.

MORN

A grove of trees, silent with the still
Of springtime morn;
Sunshine hazy, filtering through canopies richly green;
Shafts of purest gold, borne
Upon a calm and waiting air,
Prelude to a glory not yet there.

A grove of trees, alone,
And far enough away
To promise isolation, hope,
Solitude, and soul's respite to pray
And plead for greater light;
Spring morning's dawn, and end to darkness' night.

The grove of trees—a farmer's son
Waiting, praying, struggling with satanic foes;
And then, infused with light beyond degree,
Unearthly glory, peace, serenity:
Young Joseph kneeling in the grove alone—
In answer, two appear: the Father and the Son.

The Sacred Grove ... the Father's Voice:
"This is my beloved Son, hear Him!"
Joseph's mortal senses basking in the radiance of Gods,
Perceiving Truths sublime (corrupted by the whim
And sacrilegious infamy of countless generations),
Commanded then: "Restore the Truth to erring nations."

The Sacred Grove, monument
To one who offered all—
His life, his soul—in service of His God,

Of Christ, Who through His offer burst the thrall
Of sin, of ignorance, of death;
A Grove, and whisperings of godly breath.

The Gospel in the Latter Days

A window box cramped
above meshed
blue-steel bands
of smog

(Homestead diminished
to a rented apartment
and a single cubic yard
of earth.);

a tomato vine
sprinkled with fruit—
green, red, ripening yellow—
twines outside a kitchen window;
its branches are heavily laden
and

a two-inch green caterpillar
clutches tenuously
a leaf
arching empty space.

One cubic yard of earth—
and an enemy.
Yet there will be a harvest still.

Prelude

How soon must I commence the work
To which I feel myself compelled—
An impulse urging, as a river
Flooding from its source, unquelled.

'Tis ever so, as testified
And read in prophets' words revealed,
When God empowers a human voice:
'Unveil to men My Words concealed.'

But I, a youth! How could I know,
Suspect that I should fill a part
In His Immensity of Love;
O task beyond mere reasoned art.

Yea, He commands; therefore I know
That strength and wisdom and delight
In serving Him devolve on me;
He so commands, and I so write:

    I, Nephi, having been born....

DOUBLE QUOTELLA

"That They Might Not Cross
the Great Waters in Darkness" (Ether 6:3)

That was God's requirement — through darkness
They must cross, to light must cross, in

Might of Christ Unborn. Yet on green shores (waters
Not yet touched by sandaled feet) they shivered fear as if a great
Cross at the vision of dreadful blackness immured in the
(the God-inspired) barges. They questioned how they could cross
Great silences without sight. And they would not.
Waters, yes — but through God's might

In *light*. And Jared's brother prayed that they
Darkness might defy. And there was light ... and more than that.

That They Might Not in Darkness Cross
Ether 4-6

> "On a long journey of human life, faith is the best of companions; it is the best refreshment on the journey; and it is the greatest property." — Buddha

Smooth,
Cool,
Translucent almost,
Veined opal white
And burnished
By seasonal vicissitudes
Beyond all human count—
Wind, water,
Roiling gritty sand,
Ice expanding, contracting
Its rhythmic breath—

Smooth,
Cool,
Lying unnoticed, useless,
Until molten,
Transformed to sixteen spheres
Of glassed transparency

Common stones
Undistinguished in their creation
Until worked by man
And touched by God:
Glowing
In a self-sufficiency of Light.

"AND MY FATHER DWELT IN A TENT"
—1 Nephi 2:15

Something about tents encourages
Faith…:

That wayward winds will not wrench ragged skin from
Thin-wood bones, revealing our blunt
Nakedness;

That beating torrents will not deluge our
Goods, reaping riots of corruption,
Mold, and rust;

That elemental incandescence will not devour our
Flesh, scorch lidless eyes until they
Will not see;

That solid earth will not resume mud-
Glazed illusions lurking to impede, to
Swallow us.

"And my father dwelt in a tent"—
Something about tents enheartens
Faith.

PSALM—2 NEPHI 4: 16-35

Nephi — Prophet, Seer,
Shepherd to a tiny herd of Israel's chosen Sheep;
Young,
But with the death of agéd Lehi
Thrust into the fore —
Guardian of the fold.

Barely is the sorrowful bier
Entrusted to the beckoning earth —
No sooner than the prophet-father's breath
Sleeps, stilled by age and suffering's weight —
Than once again Rebellion's
Killing venom steals its way
To poison all — at least to try —
Against the leadership of God's appointed.
Laman, Lemuel, dead Ishmael's sons,
Once more rejecting, scorning,
And defying
God-given powers and rights.
Yet in this crucial moment —
In solitude through father's parting,
And agony for brothers' souls
Feared lost —
Pours from Nephi's valiant self
His psalm of Life and Hope:

> *"Behold, my soul delighteth*
> *In the things of the Lord."*

With what surpassing joy
Does Nephi utter this most simple phrase:
For him, it is true.
And as he speaks in subsequent,

More beauteous lines
Of poetry, the glory and the strength
Of Nephi's powerful faith
Overwhelm his sin-filled readers
And bring to recollections
The pettiness of problems that we face.

We have not left homes behind
Forever,
Abandoned our accustomed life,
The joys,
The luxuries of wealth,
To journey in the wilderness
On the strength of dreams;
Nor have we suffered
Turmoils and travails of desert life,
Of hate, and sorrow,
And of death — of separation
From the only earthly one
To understand and fully to appreciate.
Others have, yes ... perhaps ...
But we have not!

Then how dare we not feel shame
For weaknesses and our complaints,
And tears of hopeful gratitude
That knowledge of our shame
And of our Path to Restoration
Is granted us
As we read,
Understand,
Vicariously experience
The workings of the Spirit
On Nephi's eager soul.

Rejoice, o my heart! and Sing!

"I will cry unto my Lord
Forever,

For He hath seen me in the depths
Of mine afflictions;
And in His Mercy hath He led me
To this Psalm,
This balm,
To calm
And soothe
And lead me back to Faith!"

PARABLE—3 NEPHI 8-11

Storm clouds gathering, looming over crags,
Sweeping through dark, densely wooded vales,
Obscuring from the sight of earthly eyes
Blue heaven's glory.
Icy snow, wicked-white, beating,
Stinging accompaniment to wind,
To lightning's thundering spark.
Snow, shrouding remnants of dead summer's growth;
Higher, higher ... piled embankments
Drifting over mountain paths —
Treacherous enough when clearly seen,
Broken now by drifting, freezing fingers —
Snow, destroying the paths of men.
Streamlets leveled by the mass
Of solid white, not to be distinguished
From smooth meadows,
Both now alike in altitude and inclination,
Save where the fleecy billows dash
Against some lone protrusion,
Creating from the level places mounts.

Higher yet. all signs of life now hidden,
Buried beneath the thick and smothering cloak
Of silent snow
(Beneath it, all is black and dark,
No shafts of light to penetrate,
To warm and thaw the freezing loam).

Then as a flash, a darting ray
From Springtime's harbinger, the sun,
Shatters darkness' bands;
Calls clarion-clear — announces

To a frozen world cold Winter's end.
Rebirth and life anew descending
From the sun to thaw and warm
The earth with rays of life;
And, as if personified, reflects
The vibrant being of its source
In a single golden Crocus cup;

The Sun of Heaven
Springing forth upon the earth,
Clothed in earthly glory,
Messenger of coming Light and everlasting Life.

The darkness and the cold are past;
Within the mountain vales comes life anew.

The Faithful Behold the Risen Christ
For Lawrence Jeremy Jensen

I was blind from birth;
A sightless face peering blankly
                        Into life,
Hoping ever once to see.
With ears
        And hands
I sought to see my world,
Shape its forms within my mind.
As a child,
My father told me of the light,
                  Of sun,
                  Of moon,
                  Of stars,
That I could never see.
He drew their outlines in the dust
And with his roughened hands
Would guide my own
Along the tiny furrows:
"This, with points, a star;
This, the crescent moon
Curving through the sky."
As he would work the land by day,
I would sit in night
Beside my mother's voice.
I listened as she spoke of sunsets,
                  lakes,
           and rivers;
And I would feel a fragrant softness
As she showed me through my fingertips
The flowers of our yard.

She told me stories of the past:
        Of our fathers' journeys from the East;
              Of wars,
                      Of trials,
And of the Prophecies.
She told me of the Star
That blossomed forth that night
In answer to the prophecies of holy men;
Of how she, when a child, stood awed,
Aware of the greatness of that night.
My years were spent in darkness,
Waiting.

Then came the time of trembling
        And of shock within the earth,
              And cries,
                      And tears,
                            And sounds of desolation.
They say that there was darkness—
I felt a strangeness on my cheeks,
A heaviness of air
That stifled breath.
They say three days of that
Before again the sun broke forth.
Three days, when I could see
To guide my parents through the ruins
Of our home.
My hands and feet
Could see the paths to water, food,
And bring them back to those
Whose sudden blindness
Stilled their limbs
And hopes.
I, and I alone,
        Could see;
                Could serve instead of being served.
In the darkness, I was whole.
I felt a purpose to my life.

Then rose the sun upon my blindness,
Warmth upon my flesh,
Darkness in my eyes—
But strangely different.
The air was tinged with expectation.
  Something had occurred,
  Something marvelous.
I remember sounds of mourning
Mingling with sounds of joy;
Hurried words of Signs and Prophecies,
Of Him whose death
Had caused the earth's recoil
And darkness' veil to drop
Upon the land.

Time passed.
They worked to build our homes,
Those whose lives were spared.
My parents had no leisure now
To sit beside their blind-born child
And smooth the tumbling hours
With their tales.
They worked with diligence,
They found small tasks that I could do;
And yet I knew their love for me
Had deepened in the darkness;
I knew that He
Of whom they often spoke
Had wrought a change within our lives
Through His death.

Then came the day.
The morning sweetness lingered long,
Soothing where the sun's first rays
Fingered warmly on my head
And lid-closed eyes,
    Peaceful,

                    Calm….
A swift, soft step
Up to my parents' door;
Whispered words ...
And we set forth,
I in darkness,
Down the twisted paths
That led us to the temple's gates.
I heard the voices' quiet tones
Relating marvels,
        Miracles,
                And hopes.
I heard the voices
I had heard from birth,
Now softened and subdued.
Then silence—
As a Voice above me spoke,
High above,
Within those Heavens I had never seen.
I could not understand the words,
Yet sensed their gentle love
And breathless strength.
Again the Voice;
The third time,
And I, a child, a small, blind child
Who had listened to the teachings
Of a mother's voice
And had believed them all;
I, a child, could understand
                As God announced
                        The coming of His Son.
I heard ...
    But could not see!

What Christ spoke
I did not comprehend.
I only heard His Voice
    And knew it was of Love.

I sat within the circle of His voice
        And knew not blindness,
                Loneliness,
                        Or fear.

I heard him speak,
Then stop.
I felt His gaze upon my soul.
He spoke again:
Behold, my bowels are filled
With compassion toward you.
Have ye any
That are sick among you?
Bring them hither.
Have ye any that are lame,
Or blind,
Or halt,
Or maimed,
Or leprous,
Or that are withered,
Or that are deaf,
Or that are afflicted in any manner?
Bring them hither
And I will heal them
For I have compassion upon you.
My bowels are filled with mercy.

My mother's trembling hands
Upon my arm,
Guiding me.
Warm tears dropping,
Tiny splashes on my flesh.
I walked to Him.
      He touched my eyes,
           He searched me with His fingertips,
         He whispered:
    Look at me.

I raised my head,

My eyes,
And looked into the whiteness of His face.
I was blind from birth;
He touched me,
And I see!

Reading "The Faithful Behold the Risen Christ"
For Judi

Rising from the solemn silences
One note, then two, then full piano chords
Swell, crescendo, dim before her voice,
Velvet voice and mellow with sweet tears
Swirling dreams of midnight-silver waves
Caressing sandy stretches with phosphorescent glimmerings;

She reads on, becoming for a moment's span
A birth-blind Nephite girl; and blindness-seeming
Darkens star-deep eyes of those who hear.
The thunder of destruction startles hearers,
Shaking them from silent reverie,
Leading from the earthquakes, tempests,
To blackness, unseen terrors crouching near,
Eyes long blind alert to nuances
Of sound and shape (I cannot see;
The hand-scrawled notes are blurred and hesitant).

Then once again, that clover-honey voice,
Speaks of *Christ*, of words, of gentle hands
Upon dark sockets — speaks of vision's light!
My left hand spiders from the bass toward
Soprano tones, notes fading, fading, still ....

And I, and she, and all breathe reverent joy
And, throat-choked, weep our happiness.

ON THE ROAD TO BOUNTIFUL

Red sun, red-filtered through slant shafts of dust,
Portends the end of night-time's journey's toils
On the road to Bountiful.

With crushing blast the storm first broke
In anger—earthquakes ripped our land
And darkness filled our hearts with terror;
Tears our eyes, suffering our ears.

For three days, until arose
The sun upon a broken soil
Twisted, wrenched beyond all pain:
Yet peaceful in a waiting calm.

Twilight words, and whispered toil
Along fractured paths by dark.
Hasten! Hasten! through the wastes
Toward the glimmerings of this dawn.

Hills like broken crusts are steeped in wine
From morning's vatic rays, on the road
To Bountiful ... to greet the golden Son.

. . . AND MY TRUTHS FAILED

I am a Poet,
Or, rather, was;
Once, when I was young,
I dipped my pen in midnight ink
And from the point flowed
Vast visions of Eternity:
Tales of Prophets and of Prophecies,
Marvels, and great Miracles;
Parchment sheets became
Broad battlefields,
With ink-sketched warrior-armies
Sweeping over blood-drunk lands
As grey-frothed waves retreat
Toward the sea
To surge again with crushing power
Upon the long-withstanding shores.
Or sometimes scenes of sorrow
And of fear
Found egress from my inner world,
And great men bowed
Beneath dark chains
As wickedness incarnate—
And stupidity—
Attempted to pervert
The Revelations' laws,
While Righteousness stood firm
Within the fires
Of sin's consuming blaze,
Triumphing though in death.

In other times,

The beauties of the world
Enticed my martial thoughts toward
More gentle slopes
And mountain glens;
Bursting streams cascading to escape
Cold winter's crystal casements;
Summer, fall, and winter once again
In rhythmic sequence
Flourished, ripened,
Died into the cycle.
As words took form
Upon the empty sheets,
I descended to the depths of pain
And sorrow,
Then winged in exultation far beyond
To revel in rich ecstasies of joy
And godly happiness.
Through Poet's eyes this world appeared
A place divinely formed,
For man endowed with hope, challenge,
And felicity.
I endeavored to express those Truths
Which Prophets see and Poets feel—
Until the Truths of Poets failed.

He came.
And all was changed.
Prophets' glints
And Poets' feeble lights
Were as nothing when He came.
No metaphor could comprehend His Voice;
His words more meaningful and true
Than Truths that paved the way
For Him.
The Prophets spoke no more,
And Poets shared the reverential still;
For who would speak
When He,

Whose Being far surpassed reality,
Was near;
Who would bare the world's soul
While kneeling in the presence of
The Universal One,
The world's self-Metaphor.

Perhaps some time,
Later,
When our common memory of Him
Must be passed on
To others not alive when He was here,
Prophecy shall resurrect
With Poetry,
And the inner world of Truth
Shall live anew;
Perhaps when we once more must speak,
Express the inexpressible,
The realm of man and nature will allow
Analogies to Him
Who both Nature is and Man—
And of them God.
Perhaps ....
But yet I sit in silence,
For all now know what I would speak,
Those half-Truths
Which we flattered once as whole,
No more the sole reserve
Of Prophets and of Poetry;
The greater Truth,
Which all may see and understand,
Is with us through His light.

I am a Poet,
Or, rather, was,
Once, when I was young in years;
But now, when I am young in Him,
My Truths have failed,

For I have his;
I am no more,
Because He is.

On Arnold Friberg's *Mormon Bids Farewell to a Once Great Nation*

Beneath a single red-gold leaf
Clutching tiredly at its branch,
An unarmed arm reaches out
Toward the masses—dead and dying—
Of the decimated;
Leaf and arm in stark relief
Against a sodden, threatening sky
Overcast with bloody calm.
From this lonely, deathly prospect
Overlooking massacre
And death, the old one lies, supported
By the image of his flesh;
Weakened not by marching years,
But by the mortal wounds of trial
After half a century—and more—
Of war, defeated by searing sins of those
Whose lives he sought to save,
Whose pride and wickedness conspired
To pierce his aging flesh, and theirs collectively.

Black carrion-birds descend upon
And ravage stiffening bodies cold.
White and red, in death combined,
Uniting broken limbs and souls.
They have ceased their senseless struggles,
Vanquished by the Adversary's guiles.
But one has won internal victory;
For in his shrouded grasp he clasps
The Plates of Gold, of value beyond gold—
Graven record of this passing folk—

The plates, addressed to generations
He should never live to see
But which he knows must surely come
And war with remnants of his own,
Reveal salvation to his own.

In blood-streaked sunset glow he rests,
Breathes a silent benediction
On the dead. His face reflects
The glare of dying day.
Behind, the son awaits, prepared
To take upon himself the sole
Responsibility of love.
Unmoving, still, the arm extends
In final gesture of farewell,
The arm of man that served the Arm of God.

Above, a single red-gold leaf,
Last of multitudes,
Clutches at its bough.

THE STEWARD

**For Lawrence Jeremy Jensen
Michael Gailey
and other Elders of the
Germany North Mission
1969-1971**

They come. I hear them rustling dying leaves,
Imagine dark and glistening bodies unclothed
Except for savage paints and rudely tanned robes
To protect raw, naked redness from winter's frost.
I imagine them as they draw near, surround,
Exclude all possibility of escape.

Escape!
      For me!
            What need I
                  To escape?
I laugh almost—and weep—
To contemplate the fear immobilizing
Darkened souls ... fear and hate of wickedness
For good; fear that has encaptivated,
Bound for twenty years and more bold warriors,
Victors of our last encounter.
They fear dead Mormon, gentle father,
Intrepid general, who led his damnéd folk
So valiantly. Still ringing in my ears ....
      Fevered triumph and hellish turmoil
      As they cut him down,
      Stained our red and sodden land
      With prophet's guiltless blood.
How near I came to hatred! O my father!

They fear dead Mormon, and dead Mormon's son,
Ghost-grey, silent wanderer whose steps
Have foiled two decades drear of persecution
And of loneliness. But more than these,
They dread and hate immortal words inscribed
Upon my precious plates sealed safely in
Silent bowels of earth. Now I must wait
But moments more for my release. I tire.
I lie and wait.

I've seen so much in my long life, and all
Has gone. I remain, alone. Here,
By my side, my weapons: Stylus,
Tools that once engraved my father's words
Deep into thin plates of gold. Those plates ...
How closely to theirs has my fate been bound!
Before my birth my father took into
His care the sacred manuscripts, protected
Them, preserved them, until at death's
Approach relinquishing his Stewardship.
The plates—my link with past and hope for
Future joys.

How strange it was, that first time, long ago;
Sealing up the records in their vault,
Burying my testimony for
An unborn world. I prepared myself to die,
Pierced by silent arrow's point while skirting
Through dark forest shadows; slain by sword
Sustained by unseen foe. I left the mount,
The scene of fearful carnage and sad death,
To seek my lonely end in wooded vales
Of this once Promised Land.

But still I know no peace, no sudden, searing
Pain to rend the veil twixt here and now
And those I long to see.

                              No peace....
But deep within, a gnawing impulse guiding
Me in one great round until I find
Myself again surveying gruesome signs
Of death that I had hoped forever to
Forget. I steal toward that single spot
Which they must never find:
        Darkness' shelter, mercifully shielding
        Wanderer's gaze upon warrior-graves,
        Sparing sight of battle-remnants:
        Ravaged corpses, carrion for ravens;
        Familiar forms, shadowed in death.

Moving steadily, forced to tread into
Still realms of death and silence chill avoided
By blood-painted victors since that time
Long lives ago; gliding through broken bones,
Bent armor of what once had been my fellow
Men. With each careful step drawn closer
To my goal and destiny: The Plates!
Reverent hands removing them; retiring
Into that sheltered niche known only to
The ordained Writers of the Histories;
And there to work for days,
                      or hours,
                                or weeks
(Time's passage has no meaning now)
Until again ... again ...
The record seems complete lies is re-sealed,
Entrusted to the secret earth to
Wait his generations yet to come.
No more sustained by the immediacy of work,
I wend my faltering way waste wilds,
My unsure paths transport me from this place of woe
And of salvation's vision's promises.

Through many season's cycles still alone
I wander—living death. In every face

The countenance of one who seeks to end
Eternally this mortal state of mine.
A day,
         or two,
                  or several in one place;
Then I depart to seek abode more sure,
Away from searching, prying, darkness' eyes;
Seeking repose, but finding it...
                        ...not yet.
For ever burns that subtle spark of old,
Foreknowledge of great labors unfulfilled.
I know I must return once more.

The years flown by have greatly altered landscapes
Near the hill. Winter's powdered gleaming
Buries for this one short season bones
Still undisturbed throughout the hallowed vales.
But here and there lie evidence that they
Now dare to venture through the scene of sorrow,
Pillaging and plundering that
Which for long years remained untouched.
My pounding blood reveals anxiety
As I approach the glade upon the mount,
See that they have been here, too.
                        The stone ...
It is unmoved, and there beneath, deep-sheltered
In fast-frozen earth, repose the plates,
The written remnant of my folk.
A second time they quit the velvet blindness
Of their vault to venture forth; and with them
Now the Holy Stones, Interpreters,
For I append to current tragedy
Another tale, stamp into malleable ore
The story of the first great slaughter around
This hill, pre-dating ours a thousand years.
From other plates I draw my words, as written
By an outcast such as I to warn of
Evil's consequence and darkness' secret sins.

O, had my people listened to our words.

Done. The solemn story now addendum
To my people's history, the plates
Relinquished once more to the earth.
                              And I
Depart into my solitude, abandon
Battle-memories, fields where winter's
Melting, silvery blood flows coldly over
Rusted relics and decay of warfare
Fully half a generation gone.
Done. The book complete. Yet I survive
From day to day. I know not why, though surely
He in His high wisdom has a purpose
Here on earth that I may yet fulfill.

Winter once again, again, and still
Again. With each wheeling, passing season
Intensifies the knowledge deep:
I must return.

The third time—spring. Pale earth re-clothed in garbs
Of green, of life, of joy. The year's new growth,
Its vibrant colors hide mute witnesses
To past despair, sanctify old bones
In living sepulchers ablaze with scents.
The hill remains the same, thrusting over
Lowland plains, stalwart sentinel
Guarding its secret trove.
Strange, but here white blossoms seem to nod
More solemnly, their beauty muted and subdued
To match this mountain's sacred character.
The stone—first set in place by these old hands
Before they bore the scars and signs of age
And toil (before they ceased to be my hands
And transformed into my father's well-known hands
As I remember them from when I was a child);
The stone—covered then so carefully

With sod to hide it from revengeful searchers' view.
The stone—now twice removed, now twice reset,
It looks as if it has steadfastly stood
On that one spot since time and history began.
The stone—the vault:
> Rich blessings, bounteous land;
> Joy and prosperity, sin and pride,
> Terror, tragedy, human tears
> Recorded clearly; cold metal
> Plates of gold, gleaming treasure
> Earth-entrusted, buried silently.

They've not yet murdered me.
I must write more.

Empty.
        Weak.
                Alone as never before
In all the years of lengthening loneliness.
It's different now; I know my end is near.
I thought so, often, earlier, but now
I know.
My duty here is with this act fulfilled,
My tale is told; there can be nothing more
To say.

At last the peace I seek is mine.
My final mortal testimony
Lies concealed with other ancient
Holy records deep within
Dark caverns in the hill. My work,
My father's noble work is done.
I am at rest. And yet I feel
An emptiness—hollow, filled
With just that void that ever has
Accompanied the culmination
Of divine decree.
A hollowness—as if some special force
Had been removed; as if celestial

Shields have now been lowered; as if,
Before,
I could not die until the Book
Lay sealed, concealed, and hidden.
But now ....I long for my
Release, to join my father
And report my acts
Of Stewardship.

They come. I hear more plainly now:
Grate of stone beneath naked, treading feet;
Swish and scrape as autumn twigs give way
Before the forward thrust of painted arms ....
Nearer now. Murmurings subdued. Brothers'
Voices tinged with fear, uncertainty,
Almost an awe,
For something they have hated and have feared
For one full generation.

                          They come—To set
Me free. What need I fear? Or seek escape?
They enter—I close my eyes in sleep.
O, my father …
            …My God!

The Final Vision

A vast and hollow echo moans
Across wide plains—dry, barren plains
That seem to bound infinities
Of time and space immutable;

While from the oaken tribal limbs
Falling leaves of scarlet cold
Disperse until but few remain
To grace the graceless dying year.

An echo from the past, of glory
And delight, seeks its beginnings,
Sends out reverberations, seeking
Ears long deaf to commoner sounds.

But quietly the somber stretches
Await resurgences of hope,
As visions of great promises
Unfold unto the scattered ones

Fallen from the majesty
Of former heights. Throughout the wastes
Moist winds propel the soothing voice
Of rising and regeneration.

And centuries pass into the void,
Till in the fullness of all Time,
Branches bear again their burden,
And plains arise in fertile, blossoming peace.

The Dionysian Hierarchy First Notices Moroni and His Friends

Wing-warped angels pause, look askance
at wingless forms new formed,
hover-clustering beneath a sterile

moon. They pause, deign a glance
from heaven's Seventh Sphere,
and murmur: "Latecomer Imps! Puerile

afterthoughts! Scrabbling for a chance
encounter with Mortality!"
They pause, and flare sheer wings with feral

grace—not noticing that their Cosmic Dance
stutters to a vacuous close ...
forgetting metaphor to their mythic peril.

ON THE EVENING OF HER 95TH YEAR
For Susan Eva Barker Hurd

Spoon by patient spoon
We fed her chicken-noodle soup.
While—white hair matted, pressed flat—
She sipped and rasped and coughed, stoop-
Shouldered, trembling—chilled beneath
Quilt blocks she stitched sixty years before.

We fed her chicken-noodle soup,
Careful to mince the noodles,
Space them carefully in the spoon.
We touched her lips with a paper napkin's
Edge—her chin, a spot in her frayed
Housedress where a single drop

Had left a glistening, oily spot.
She sipped. She rasped and coughed.
Sipped again. And when I touched
Her forehead for some sign of fever
Or of chill, she leaned against my shoulder
As if she were a mother's child again.

PHOTOGRAPHS

Firmly pressed between
        glassy sheets
                my nine-year-old son

grimaces at his
        sister in
                soft shade of cotton-

woods at Lion's Camp.
        I turn the
                page to see him stand-

ing near the apri-
        cot at twelve,
                newly dressed in God

and now a Deacon;
        I turn the
                page to see him stand-

ing in the dark mouth
        of a beast
                to wing him southward

for two years, where he
        will grow in-
                to manhood and I

will have no pages
    to turn, no
            photographs to mount

LINES FOR A NEWLY RELEASED BISHOP
For Edgar Bolton

Tonight, you came to bless us in our home,
To Father-Bishop with healing oil and prayer,
As so often you have quietly done.

But tonight, there was a difference. Where
There had been solemnity, a weight
Invisible but present in the air,

Tonight…a lightness, a silent joy — a freight
Of imminence dissipated, and in
Its place quick laughter, calmness, and a sleight

Of smile that spoke acceptance. Tonight the thin
And unseen mantle you have worn for long, long
Years had slid aside; underneath, when

You rested hands on my daughter's head along
With me, I felt and heard and blessed your inner song.

On Becoming a High Priest

It's childish, I suppose, to feel
A sense of loss already—
As if another's hands could slight the real

Lineage extending back to birth
And blessing, through baptism, into Deacon,
Teacher, Priest, and Elder. The worth

Of ordination should not be counted
By the hands, the power of Priesthood
Not established by who mounted

First the summit of my head,
Pressed fingers into rough-combed hair,
And, pausing for the Spirit, said

The words that changed me from mere boy
Into a vessel-implement of God.
I should not feel a loss. This is no toy

To be distorted by who held it last;
This is more. And memory,
That warns me I should hold on fast

To that one lineage, must fall before
Understanding—for if
My father's hands are still and can no more

Press down their priesthood weight,
Another father's might; and lift
Me with my father to a higher state.

MISSION CALL
For Aaron Riggs

When he said Dresden my heart arrested and
I saw in atom-flash Erika Schumacher's tears
as she turned brittle pre-war pages
and pointed with arthritic fingers
at buildings that once were and were no more—
She wept for Dresden.

I hoped that he would say Hamburg and
I could share sharp photographs,
twenty-four-year-old transparencies
of St. Peter's stone and St. Michael's weathered spires,
and hope that he might sit in Altona
or Wartenau, where I once sat.

But Dresden ....
I cannot imagine Dresden—
deep inside the Eastern Zone when I was there,
immense beyond the Wall, beyond the West,
beyond the Binnenalster that sheened familiar,
whose well-tamed shores tasted smelled felt American—

But Dresden—
brittle as china shards weeping in bright sunlight,
fragile as slivered porcelain curves
buried in lake mud by unforgotten bombs ...
mystery behind the
Wall-non-Wall.

Dresden ...
to be there, to build where firebombs destroyed,
to build what will not pass or burn or fail,
to build when years begin to pale
and warfires burn to ash of
memory—and new fires kindle

ignite sweep flash
across the spirit of rebuilt walls
rejoined East to West in physical landscape and
bonds of newly breathed belief—
and he will midwife wonders from the spark of
Dresden ....

ORDINATION

Beneath rough hands, a
curve of bone concealed
by thick dark hair arcs
out and down where once
an infant softness
cradled in my hand
as I drew breath and
spoke another set
of words to give you
name and bless your new
beginnings.
                        Now these
words march harsh and slow
between trembling lips,
hover on a tongue
that has flashed out in
anger, spat retorts,
hesitated in
dark silent stretches
of questing sleepless
nights.
                    Lips and tongue form
unfelt sounds, taste hot
salty syllables
savioring the change
that lays forever
into memory
your infant softness,
marks your passage to
an awe-full power

we now discover
hand in hand as one.

ISLANDS
In Memoriam:
Bryan and Monte Bolton
January 5, 1992

From the shore, the Channel Islands mound
Indistinctly grey against grey skies;
Barely separate from waters that surround,

They rest like invert wombs. Sheer turrets rise
At Cathedral Point—but we cannot see
Such detail from our shore. It strains our eyes

Just to trace dark, arcing curves of scree
That mark sharp land from mapless ocean ways.
Cloud-shrouded, the islands keep their mystery

From those of us on shore. Their lead-grey bays
And coves hide secrets frightening and dark;
Beneath thick storm-whipped spray and dusky haze,

The islands terrify. Their outlines mark
Blind boundaries of our human, mortal vision.
Grey shapes, they stand stark symbols of the dark,

Of loss, of harsh unbearable collision—
Love with Faith. To live without the Love ...
Unthinkable; to endure the indecision

Loss implies ... impossible. Above
Deep mist-grey mounds, cloud cover billows, parts
For one sufficient moment. Like a dove
Of sheerest light, the sun breaks through with darts

That glance from rock to sea and back again.
A gleam...a fragment light...then gone.... But hearts

That wear the weight of grief and twisting pain
Reach up, entwined with that faint light—rebound
With faith and love to rest on Heaven's plain:

Barely held by waters that surround,
Infinite blue beneath celestial skies,
Seen from our shores, the Channel Islands mound.

MOVING ON
ELEGIACS

Quietly solemn, the chapel lies empty. Its windows glow dim grey—
Pale in the lingering dusk. The long shadows give way—
Darkness succeeds the faint glimmers of light as it swallows the last
   gleam;
Music that echoed is silent…and grief, but a harsh dream.

Empty and voiceless, the gravesite lies silent. Crisp oak leaves spin
   gold-brown,
Covering turf not yet rooted and growing. From hills, down
Sweeping on breezes still icy with winter, the Piper's soft breathing
Mingles with roses relinquished there, wilting and wreathing.

Somberly muted, the table awaits him. A missing place, there laid
Only in memory, invites him to enter. Grace said,
Heads raise, and eyes twining whisper soft sorrow unspoken, while
   slight sounds
Settle the silence his absence enforces—grief found.

Kneeling beside the thick counterpane, kneeling in prayer-still, they
   wait—
Wordlessly waiting until, like faint brush strokes they feel fate
Sealing their neediness, healing their hollowness, dulling their sharp
   pain—
Finally, sleep whispers that Unity surely shall come again.

Throbbing in rhythms mechanic but vital, lone hearts speak in loud
   beats.
Quick nighttime noises restore fractured senses. In deep dreams

Voices long silent appeal to the dreamers; the dead re-assemble,
Escort a newcomer soul. In deep dreams, tears tremble.

ON THE GROUNDS OF THE MANTI TEMPLE

Lovers' hearts incised in snow —
    Ephemeral — should blur with heat
        And melt and fade to gritty scabs
            Of ragged snow across
Dead winter's wounds.

But here they melt by day and freeze
    Again by night — and snow-heart ridges
        (Ice beneath a froth of snow)
            Outlast cold drifts beneath
Blue-shadowed pines.

REVELATION
For Brent Robinson

Perched naked on a ledge of bloodbright rock
Above a limpid eye of liquid light.
The mountain's breath caresses heavy flesh—
Legs and arms and shoulders grow refreshed
Again—steadied by the rest to fight
Further in ... further up the trail. No clock

Apportions jagged bites of frantic earthbound Time—
No inkroped map constrains my naked footfalls' tread.
I stand alone. Piercing silence drowns my ears
With music long inaudible. I weep deep tears
Of sound—rustle of pine, low whirrr of red-
Quilled hawk-tail feathers. Silent sounds that mime

Cold fire that pinions, burns, transforms an odd
Dust-driven path to ribbon-shimmering light.
I walk alone. I hunger. Thirst.
I nearly faint. I know first-
Hand the pain of transmutation—fight
All unaware the infiltrating Truth of God.

FOR THY SAKE

I spaded in the garden again today,
Adam being in the fields to husband wheat.
So I spaded in the garden, remembering
Eden: roses twining glossy ivy on
A smooth oak trunk, such massed perfumes
That I could scarcely stand. Or apricots
And peaches, gold and blush, bowing stiff-spined
Branches earthward. I needed merely look,
Or pluck and eat, or smell.

And tomorrow, I shall spade again, for now
the apricots, the peaches, and the rose
belong to me.

ON THE LAST DAY OF HER DYING

On the last day of her
dying pain crocheted
taut nerve-knots
too tight
for lifeblood
to unravel

Breath
drew ragged
razorcuts
through lungs
and throat
while

fingers burned
with icy heat
and taloned sheets
too smooth
to shroud
her brittle husk

In the last instant of her
dying pain-blood-ice
mounted
shuddered
climaxed
and released

a flush
of light and

oh-cool-quiet
rest

BAPTISM—AS LIGHT AS SNOW

Cool, waist-high,
      shallower than remembered:
              eight years ago, it seemed
that I would float.

Now, water shallower,
      less buoyant to my gravity,
              I descended first (my first),
reached out.

Spoke. An uncracked voice
      (at last!) echoed in rigid angles
              from white tiles. I faltered at
a voice not quite my own.

I climbed out;
      a wet cotton hem
              brushed my fingertips;
I barely kept my footing.

It seemed that I would float beyond the font.

The Golden Chain

Paradise pendant from a golden chain
opal pendant paradise
swirling blue and green
through white cloud streaks:
golden chain gleaming on the breast of God.

But now

The chain hangs empty
Earth has fled to embrace darkness

and the golden chain
long-line smooth, sun-linked
and heavy with eternity

hangs empty

CREATION

First Day

but when they opened
slowly
into a deep blackness
the immensity of the abyss
overpowered.
Fear brushed his rising breast
and nothingness met his
paling gaze.
Time no longer seemed to move
except in spaced
staccato
bursts, keeping tempo
with his heart-beat-throbs.
They seemed to slash
and gash
the shroud within the room,
to see into the slivered light
between the pulsing flow,
waiting for the grey.
When it came
between the heart-beat-throbs
through the shroud
he moved.
Coldness struck his body
as bare feet crossed thick ice-oak planks,
slid toward a frost-edges square
of grey
facing white
opening upon waved crested drifts

Second Day

swirling quietly against granite walls
the wind of twilight murmured:
rest,
repose.
As he settled back
upon a tick of native fragrance
grey-gold dusk descended.
Eyes closed,
inhaling liquid light,
he lay unmoving,
floating,
rising on infinities
odoriferous;
suspended,
arms outstretched,
searching diamond thoughts
within a fevered consciousness.
In the evening calm
he felt himself expand until
like Job his coffin
suspended
between earth and sky

Third Day

watching
on the fractured rocky shore,
immersed in misty coolness
boiling through the heat
of day,
he stared into the fog
as it moved
in indiscriminate fluffs
of ragged white
upon the surface of the lake.

Its blue-grey
fluted by the fingered wing,
the lake slid slowly to the west
between twin buttresses of stone.
Like cotton-puff parades
the fogs progressed across the waters,
alternately hiding
then exposing
distant blue-tinged peaks.
He stared into the fog,
probing.
He stared and dreamed

Fourth Day

while fading sunlight
gilded pine tips
and crumbling domes of granite,
he cleared the ground.
Tiny twigs,
fragmented, weathered rocks,
cones and needles
flew before his makeshift brush.
Within the high-walled cleft,
grassless
nearly treeless,
he spread his nylon bed,
smoothing wrinkled planes.
He knelt upon the cold, damp surface
and raised his eyes
beyond the rocks
beyond the circling pines
beyond the earth
and focused on the stars of heaven.
Sunrise found him facing east
waiting for the day,
the resurrection of the sun

Fifth Day

until the night fell,
severing the spit of meadow
underneath his feet
from disappearing pines,
all was silent.
Clouds like darkened petals
swirling in pools of indigo
glided through the silences
between the flowing stars and moon
and his probing eyes.
Ink-black dropped in sheets of night
upon the peaks
the forest stretches
the lake
and finally the fleck of grassy sand
on which he stood
watching.
Behind him came a scraping sound
of granite shard on granite shard,
a softly sucking sound
as something stole across the mud
bordering the water's edge.
Something stumbled slightly
before it splashed
onto the foot-deep shelf.
He turned
to see the lowered head,
the shadow on the blackness of the night,
as the doe stretched down
to quench her thirst.
He stood
until she backed again
into the night
leaving him,
the man,
alone

Sixth Day

without speaking
they stood
sharing silent dialogue
through eye and heart,
communing in that language
understood by all.
He must leave,
she remain;
but yet no parting sorrows,
rather joys
they shared.
The hours passed in quiet
until it grew so late
and early
parting could no longer wait.
Hand to hand
palm to palm
they touched
and without words
said all that could be said.

Seventh Day

In rest,
in peace,
in joy
he lay upon his bed
and closed his eyes
in sleep

IN THE TEMPLE

Beneath the golden glow
Of upraised Trump
The cooling marble stands
Inviting,
Set amid the roses' bloom,
Grasses fine,
And fountains' singing prayers.

Within, we draw so near
And seek the Truth
Of our relationship;
In calm perfection of the halls,
White-clad figures
Moving, sharing,
Verging on Eternity.

IN CONCERT: THE ORGAN

Hand and foot
we play our Solo

Part, until
sweet music's convolutions Swell

And are revealed
deep counterpoints in God's Great

Scale, coupling all
in all-surpassing Choir.

SURROGATE: ORGANIST

With all the strength of hand, and heart, and eye,
I touch warm keys, I live the mighty swells,
I *am* high praises to His Name
And bear His Hymns in me;
Tune brass voices,
Rise in faithful majesty
And sound great trumpets in His Fame,
Make joyful echoes peal — sweet silver bells
To pierce this dome and penetrate worlds on High

DEDICATION

I was sent to serve in Paraguay,
He will bless them in their searching faith
and in their poverty, I know
                                          how blessed we are
                            To share this instrument—to hear
                         Its diapasons call, its sub-bass rumble
                                  reverential distances
                            mean more here than at home;
my companion and I walked six hours
through jungle yesterday to teach
a single family
                         of pipes requires a world of sounds—
                   Woodland flutes that call to meditative mind
                        an exhalation of sparrows in grey moments
                                  just past dawn…we pray
each day for the people here.
I have no white shirts any more—
the choking dust has turned them
featureless, dusky grey
                                              shadows hide
              Each individual voice, balanced on its wooden air-chest,
                             Hovering behind the screen
                                 Waiting for the moment
is ripe, but the people lack so much.
We would have baptized her but
she had no shoes to wear to
our makeshift chapel
                          full, church full, expectant congregation
                                                  Poised;
                           And I play prelude on an instrument
                           That cost five chapels for South America.

Dear Dad,
I love the work,
I love the people, pray every day that
They will truly hear the Gospel's words.

Playing "The Lost Chord" at Sacrament Meeting

It's a solo for organ by Arthur himself,
With no touch of Gilbertian patter—
Since no one has heard it in twenty long years,
If I make a mistake it won't matter.

I pull out the stops, the low and the high,
I brace up the music, and pray—
Then take a deep breath, check once at my feet,
Press down with four limbs ... and I play!

The organ resounds with inimitable sounds—
Rich Flutes and strong Diapasons ...
I'm lost in the notes. Ward members sit still—
And for once I don't care if I'm playsome.

I begin with the lightest of possible Flutes,
Transmuted to strong piping breaths;
But halfway along the music transforms
To the pedal Posaune's sharp depths.

I thunder and rumble through chord after chord,
Enshrouded in glorious sound—
Then stop ... hear the echo of silence divine,
And the Chord that was lost has been found.

After Thirty Years as a Ward Organist

It's still a love affair. Warm sounds wrap me
Velvetly. Strident chords shatter soul-ice
Scaffolding a rigid spinal barrier ...
A touch of music—tentative—suffices to restore.

Power flows from thee to me,
From me to thee—reciprocality ignites
Flesh, chills turgid blood, and
Smoothes like graceful oils on blistered skin.

Power flows. Thou art power; I am power.
Synergy demands power squared,
And, trembling, when I desert my place
I leave behind the better part of me.

A wrenching now three decades long enduring—
Split, torn ... hating fumbling fingers,
Clumsy feet ... but drawn obsessive, willing,
To the keys—still a love affair.

THE ORGANIST TO THE CONGREGATION

Fifteen minutes to the hour. The chapel—
Empty now—breathes graciousness. Grey carpet
Mutes my steps as I approach the height
Where keyboard, pedals, console wait for me.
An instrument ... a friend ... companion through
Long hours, long years of solitude. A lover
As my fingertips caress smooth ivory-whites,
My toes inspire a trembling, rumbling bass.
Just an instrument of metal framed in wood—
But we speak to one another's passionate blood.

Ten minutes to ....A prelude hymns its way
Above a scattering of souls silent
In deep meditative calm. I touch
A wrenching sweetness, miming forest flutes
That hover tremulant beyond my head.

Five minutes to ....We speak in soft communion
Now—the instrument, and you, and I.
Your spirit washes me. Your reverential
Quietude conjures an echo chamber
Without sound. And breathless, we are one.

The hour, minus only seconds now ....
Together we ascend with spiraled sound,
Swirl, descend to wood-grain diapasons,
Flutes ... tender airs that knit our distant
Thoughts, that link our disparate/desperate hearts,
And join our willing souls in readiness to serve.

HUMILITY IS HARD

Humility is hard since they've recarpeted
The ward in steel-grey with overtones of blue.
Oh, the carpeting is no crass problem by itself.
But when they worked the choir loft they raised the organ
By a foot almost—capped the wide recession
Where it stood and raised it 'til it thrusts its mass
Above the high-backed choir seats. It arrogates
Unto itself quiet space where once the Faithful's eyes
In wordless prayer might focus on the rough-cut native
Rock cemented roughly like a garden wall.

And I—the organist—ethereal and distant ... —
I float above the console, head and body crowning
The apex of the chapel where I greet and hush,
I welcome, re-create our Christ once crucified
New-resurrected in the Sacramental hymn.
I rouse the congregation, and I bid farewell.
And all ethereal and distanced, untouched except
By the sometimes Spirit flowing flames,
Pressing living light through livid fingertips.

Since they recarpeted the ward in steel-grey,
With overtones of heaven-blue, humility is hard.

CARILLON
For Joseph Peeples

Shell-coiled hands, delicate as feather-breath,
Flick dark, polished wood to move the clapper—
Fragile leaden sphere—a fraction-inch
To kiss curved weathered brass and—lightly—sing;

Steady-hands, tautly poised, swivel on wrists,
Strike solidly, crisply—twist—and arcing
Tones wing from the tower, feather-flight-high
Above brick and stone and wood and grass;

Hammer-hands, deftly powerful, pound
The lowest octave, pull the ten-inch weight—
Straining against gravity—two inches;
Lead rebounds from bronze in rumbling might—

And all—fragile, solid, massive—blend
In one percussive, raw, ethereal chord.

Translations from *Prayers of Solitude*
by Antoine de Saint-Exupéry

Gebet der Einsamkeit

Mercy, o my Lord, have mercy on me!
My solitude oppresses me.
There is nothing to await in life.
I sit here, in my chamber's silences,
Where nothing speaks to me.
And yet I feel no urge toward human-kind;
I know I am more lost when I'm submerged
Within the crowd. But behold the other,
Who, like me, sits in a lonely room;
She feels great joy, for those her tenderness
Supports are — somewhere — busy in her home.
She hears them not and sees them not,
Perceives no visions of their presence there.
For her to know full joy, it is enough
For her to know her home is occupied.
      Lord, I do not wish to see, or hear.
Thy wonders far surpass my senses' powers.
For my salvation, it would suffice if Thou
Infuse my spirit-mind with light, that I
Might understand my home.

Prayer for Consuelo

Lord,
It is unworthy Thou shouldst spend Thy strength
For me. Leave me simply as I am.
In small things is my vanity revealed;

Yet in the great modesty shines through.
In small things I am wrapped within myself;
Yet in the great my life is not my own
And all I have is sacrificed with joy.
In small things is impurity my shame;
Yet I am happy only when I am pure.
Lord, make me more like unto her
Whom my husband sees when he sees me;
Lord, preserve my husband, for he loves
Sincerely, and without him and his love
I am a desert waste devoid of life;
Yet, Lord, I pray that he might go before
When we in lonely death depart this life;
His strength seems great, but his deep anxiousness
Would make those years alone slow, futile ones;
He would not hear my sounds within the home.
Lord, preserve my Love from lonely anguish;
Preserve my life, that I might always make
Sounds of me within his house — just
To break a glass, a plate, from time to time.
    Help me, o my Lord, to be true
To him and that with all my will avoid
Which he in hatred and contempt disdains;
For otherwise to act would sadden him —
his life and love are wholly based in me.
Preserve, o Lord, our home.
Thy Consuelo.
                      Amen.

When I Shall Die, O Lord

When I shall die, o Lord,
I shall come to thee;
For I have ordered the tilled plot in Thy Name
    Thine is the seed.
I have formed this taper;
    It lies with Thee to light it.
I have built this temple;

It lies with Thee
To dwell within its silences.

PART THREE

Abraham's Confession of Faith

A Poetic Reconstruction from Ancient Semitic Legends

ABRAHAM'S CONFESSION OF FAITH

i

And as he spoke, the old man's voice, though strong,
Coarse and caked by desert dust, by age
And age's toil, broke;
The hearthfire near the centerpole
Seemed embrous flames deep-set in pinched black eyes.

ii

Shadows slowly marched across skinwalls
Behind us all, as we crouched low,
Straining ears to hear
Faint breathing, every nuance of his chant,
See blood-red shadows on his wrinkled brow;

iii

For even then we knew ... somehow ... that he
Would shortly pass as others had,
His knowledge speak no more;
And we in turn should be his heirs,
To plant his wisdom in yet-unborn sons.

iv

We listened carefully that night—nor feared
Wild demons' wailing as they rode
Upon dry, untamed winds;
Curling fingers, prying, probing,
Ripped tanned hides that sheltered us,

v
As if to rend, destroy frail age,
Silence ancient musings;
We listened...and he died,
Squatting there before dead coals,
Once-burning sparks clothed in dull-ash grey.

vi
We buried him in shapeless shifting sands.
Now I alone remain of those
Who heard his passing voice;
I give you now the words he spoke,
For I am old, and soon this fire must die.

vii
Give heed ... the Ancient's words must sound again:
Of Abraham the Patriarch,
First of four to stand
Against the serpent's wily guiles,
With Moses, Jesus, Muhammed—these the four.

1
Our Father Abraham, as wisdom says,
Grew miraculously from birth,
In one day as a week
In seven days as in a month,
In one month the child grew as in one year.

2
And, as the Wise Ones tell the truth, the child
Lived fifteen months within the cave,
Our sacred Cave of Lights,
Where he was born, then clothed and washed,
Anointed at the hands of Gabriel.

3
At first the infant received his nourishment

By suckling at angelic fingertips:
From the thumb, honey flowed;
From fingers—wine, milk, cream,
And water. And thus the child grew in faith.

4

With fifteen months, the child was as a youth,
Tall, and powerful of spirit,
Mind, and blossoming flesh;
Black eyes burned with the glow
Of deep-banked fires eager to burst forth.

5

From the hands of Gabriel the child
Received a robe of softest white,
Spotless purity,
Which grew with Abraham—no need
Of clothing new as his body swiftly waxed;

6

In his grasp, the child bore a smooth-hewn
Staff of golden desert wood,
A scepter for God's king;
And on his back, a cloak of black,
Woven by his mother's loving hand.

7

Thus clothed and nourished lived the man-child lone,
To no one known save in a dream
To fearful Nimrod sent;
Yet knowledge failed—his Creator's name
And worship, purpose and goal of life on earth.

8

Thus came the hour when Abraham stood straight,
Faced his mother as she sat
Upon a silken mat
(Richly brocaded arabesques
And swirling whorls of royal blue in which,

9

As she returned to the Cave of Lights
The third day, she found her infant
Warmly wrapped and safe)—
And Abraham spoke to her:
"Take me out, that I might look and see!"

10

Terah's wife bowed low and placed her hand
Within the hand outstretched to her
And walked beside her son;
Then bowing to the East she turned
And left her manchild in the wilderness.

11

Long time our father stood alone in thought,
In contemplation of the earth,
The Heavens spread above;
He looked about him at the vast
Extent of land and sky, then, kneeling, spake:

12

"O God of all, thou God that gav'st me life,
Blessed me with all Gifts and Goods,
Who brought'st me Heaven's food
And drink from the Floods of Paradise,
Thou truly art my Lord, my only God!"

13

Purple night enfolded him; he kept
His vigil, waiting for his God,
The God of Abraham;
Until the broad horizon burst
And one great point of light in grace arose,

14

A star, somewhat less bright than that which burned
Above the slaughtered innocents,
Above blood-sodden earth that moaned
When Nimrod's blades sought out the child
Whose Star proclaimed his claim on Nimrod's throne;

15

Jupiter arose, greatest of
The motile stars, and Abraham
Deep-reverenced him and sang:
"Thou art my God!" The child bowed
His head, his body sank as dead to earth,

16

Overcome by the power of Light immense
Out-sent from his supposed god;
For Abraham sought light,
The light that in the Cave of Lights
Had nourished him, sustained him from his birth.

17

Far off, two emerald-fiery eyes pursued
Phantom shapes in wild wastes
Until they found the child,
Pierced the black veil of his cloak;
A panther lithely faded through thick thorn-brush heaps,

18

Drawing nearer, silent under stars
Of pungent brilliance, stalking slowly;
And yet the man-child knew,
Felt a baleful lust in fiery breath,
Burning through deep somnolence and chill.

19

The child knew, Abraham was aware
Of crouching horrors amid black thorns—
He cried unto the star:
"Preserve me! o my God! Preserve!"
Then threw himself upon sharp, cutting sands.

20

He heard faint, crackling hints of graveled claws,
Smelled harsh rankness of a man-fed
Beast; then fresh breezes, still ....
Looking up, he saw no beast—
God praised—nor star-endiademing sky!

21

The star had set, and Abraham, perplexed,
Cried: "I cannot love that which fails!
Where art thou, my God,
My Savior from pale, jealous eyes
Of predators that haunt this desert plain?"

22

Enraged, he hurled his cloak into the night,
Repelled by its disguising hue,
Afraid whatever god
He sought would see its weakness,
Lack of trust in His all-shielding hand.

23

"God I know there is, but you not he!"
Invectives rose toward the place
Where Jupiter had sunk;
Then disappointment filled his breast,
Ice-emptiness replaced his fevered rage.

24

The youth stood tall, and walked toward the East,
Intuitive, to search for God;
He gradually perceived
Grey-outlined shadows focus crisp,
Bright-black—and Abraham beheld the moon,

25

Astarte named, and Mistress of the Night,
Silver huntress through the Sky,
Distorted large in rising;
But Abraham knew nothing of this—
He only saw ther cool, white lunar sphere

26

Rising through sky-meadows lush with stars;
He genuflected to the orb:
"This is my Lord, my God!"
Once again the youth would pray,
Raise voice unto the visible light of God,

27

For this new-shining sphere burned brighter far,
Destroying evanescent stars
With whimsical delight;
Thus Abraham recognized
The Master All of all created life.

28

Yet as he spoke, a ragged silhouette
Crested a low-piled swell
Of rock and wasted brush;
The mane-crowned beast crouched low to leap,
And Abraham fell prostrate to the moon,

29

Writhing for protection from jet claws,
Fanged ivory, red stalker's maw;
Our father prayed for life.
He sensed the leap, tensed muscles stretched
As iron javelins might propel through air;

30

He felt—almost!—deep-ripping pain, hot blood,
Bone shattered like translucent shells
Beneath cruel heels of brass;
But no! no pain…no crushing weight… .
The lion gone. The moon descending low.

31

Abraham ascended to sere heights
From whence the lion threw itself
To the desert floor; for he,
Sad youth, despaired lest he should lose
Sight and light of his new deity.

32

But too late Abraham mounted the throne
Abandoned by the tawny king;
The moon declined in death
And disappeared, thrusting all
In dark, and Abraham fell to the earth.

33

He cried: "Unless my God will truly guide
And soon manifest His being,
Idolatry be mine!
I can no other; God there is
Who bore both lion, panther from my path."

34

The boy—whose fifteen months seemed fifteen years,
So large he was of body, mind,
And soul—young Abraham
In anguished anger cast his curses
Into deep darkness, tear-stained curses wild;

35

Then darker anguish as he hurled his staff
As if a scepter abdicate,
Into dead dust and waste;
Unarmed, clothed only in his robe
Of softest, pliant white from Paradise,

36

Legs spread, feet firmly on the rocks
Overlooking waves of sand,
Hair windblown, free;
Unarmed, he placed his trust, his life
With Him who twice had proven merciful.

37

Slowly, slowly spread a saffron sea
Upon the East, fleeing stars
Drowned in ocean-light;
And, fanned with ragged fluffs of pink,
The imperial eye of day, the sovereign Sun,

38
Raised his searing crescent up to day.
Awe-filled, the man-child looked, observed,
And wept in boundless joy:
"O Greatest Light, enlighten me,
For thou, O God, art greatest of them all.

39
"I shall attend and worship thee from now
Until my final breath draws cold;
I sought for thee…and found."
Taking seat upon the point
Above all other heights, he worshipped, watched.

40
Morn's warm-sweet breath soon wore to daytime's heat,
Weltering, sweltering, fatal fire
Cast down on human forms;
Still Abraham knelt motionless,
Sure of quest, confident in hope.

41
Into the brilliant blindness of the sun
The youth impelled his spirit eyes,
Deified the Day;
To honor nature's God and his
He shared with nature desiccating heat,

42
Noon, afternoon, and eve; woven robe
Now sodden with rank sweat, now stiff
With salty offerings;
And now his god a lower arc
Began toward the West; the man-child feared.

43

Nor saw he, heard the sinuous approach,
The Serpent's scrape across coarse sands,
Toward the devotee;
Only as blue-distant hills
Encroached upon the circuit of the sun—

44

Too late!—perceived he his imperiled state,
Nor moved, but breathed a brutal prayer:
"Save, if God thou beest!"
With serpentine malevolence
The royal adder faded into rock;

45

No life, no breath, no more beneath the heel
Of Adam's seed to die, already
Lithified, stone-dead;
Scarlet lancings from the god
Signifying dual death ... and night.

46

Branching rays envermeiled western skies
As sun and day declined to rest;
Wine-red tears carved paths
Down cheeks from eyes now dimmed with pain
Of disappointment, fear, and loss of trust.

47

Yet deep unfolded secret strands of strength!
Though all had failed, still he knew
Beyond them all lay…God—
Not created images,
But source and root of all creative power.

48

"My people, I defy your godlessness,
Idolatry, and turn myself
As new believer true
To that creator of the Earth
And Heaven—no more to worship idle gods,

49

"But seek creation, not pale second-lights,
And turn me from idolatry.
I love not that which fails!"
In the waning light, his robe
Seemed stiff and harsh, caked with pagan blood;

50

Its salt-stiff coarseness scored young tender flesh,
Burned with blood of unclean rite,
Of deadly ignorance;
He ripped the sodden sweat-stained robe,
Tore it from his body, cast it off.

51

"No more I bear this skin of youthfulness,
But naked stand I, naked cry,
For revelation pray!"
New-clothed in nakedness, sweet cool,
The man awaited what should come with night.

52

Light-sun declined; Abraham enrobed
In blood-red livery first felt
A chill upon his brow;
All sunlight died; he shivered in
His nakedness; and darkness grew complete.

53

Beneath the stars, he once again seemed swathed
In purest white—flesh now urged
To highest pitch of love,
Devotion to the unseen God Who Was—
Naked invitation to that God!

54

"*Abraham*"—the man-child's blood first froze,
Then surged in wild delight. "*My Son,
Believe in me, thy God.*"
And he replied: "To Thee I come,
I give myself unto the God of Worlds."

55

Whirlwinds roared across the desert face,
Bright blazonings bejeweled skies,
Then all fell calm and dark;
Abraham stood, clothed in Adam's
Robe, mantled in the cloak of prophecy.

56

"I know Thee now, and I will search no more
Among the skies to find Thy Light."
Humbly bowing low,
He returned to the Cave of Lights
To wait his new commission from his God.

viii

"*Such were the Ancient's final words that night,
Before he died, that we night know
Our heritage as sons
Of Abraham through his firstborn,
The Wanderer, the Nomad, as we are.*

ix

I give them you—remember them, and guard
That none escape, or we must fail;
For I may speak no more.
My Master's face within the flames
Beckons me; but one request I make.

x

When cold-grey grow the ashes of this pit,
And my flame dwindled, dying, dead;
In this wise bury me:
Upon a height of rock and brush,
Naked, that I too might earn God's robe."

xi

He spoke, he sighed, and with the frail embers, died;
And I, the third, now speak his words,
The Ancient Master's words—
Himself the tenth in line-descent
From Ishmael, the Wanderer and the Prince;

xii

Long have these truths been known from mouth to mouth,
Long passed that we know Abraham,
Understand his God;
Past grows dim, legends fade,
And lives, like fires, expire in little time.

xiii

Yet Abraham survives, must survive,
In Christian lore, in our own truths
To point our way to God;
If true or no in every word,
He yet remains a witness to our God.

xiv
You, near the fire, set another branch
Upon the embers. Blow it till
The fire reaches high,
Wards off demons from my tent;
This night must I share all my truths with you.

PART FOUR

MY WITNESS AND MY TRUTH

THE TESTIMONY OF ALMA

My Witness and My Truth
The Testimony of Alma

I

Darkness impenetrable, oppressive silence.
A robed figure bearing a dim light
Partially but not dispelling quite
The thick, stifling gloom;
Only a face,
A figure draped in black.
Flickering lamplight reflects crimson
Through deep-set eyes.
Heaven's angry fires
Encapsulated
In a stillborn
Tear.

<u>Prologue:</u> Curse this midnight blackness
And sad cold slow-washing through my bones,
A bitter ocean swirling throughout time,
From which I never may escape—nor wish to,
Since my conscious choices in mortality
Have suited me to no existence other.
Proximity to life-preserving warmth
Would sear me now,
Enflame my essence with bright rays.
 I am summoned here to light the way—
This faint, painless fire lifts sable veils
To grey as I illuminate dark deeds
Performed long centuries before,
Now seeming to recur before your eyes—

And mine—in expiation for the darkness
That I served and loved...
Which bound my flesh and now consumes my soul.
    That it is I who comes, I argue not.
Someone must. Who better than myself
To serve a Prologue to these scenes well-known;
I, who fed hot lusts, shared secret crimes
Committed in the past, and know my error
And my shame.
But must I rush in urgent haste,
Midway between wan dusk and blooming dawn?
Could not the King convene his priestly court
Beneath the glowing powers of the day,
Instead of seeking shelter in the night
For covert crimes disguised as Justice and
Legality.
    No, deeds of darkness flourish in the night.
This blackness wears its ink-cape well for what
Now comes. I cannot hope for joy
In what I bring—what we together see....
Death only, violence, and fear becloud the scene.
To me it is not given to dispel those mists
And transcend beyond to joy and light.
    This cold! This polar-chill within my flesh!
Darkness cowls my paling flame,
Ceremental shrouds obscure my light.
I relinquish soon this narrow breath
To greater passions than I own.
I have but played my part;
They now appear whose tale we see,
Conjured from the distant past
To breathe and speak and walk
As if today were yesterday reborn.
    I am glad to fade.
Fear of Noah and his cohort priests
Infects my breast, fear that they again
Might draw me to their doom;
And I would hasten from this temple-court,

From this cold chamber glistening with gold,
Where power riots in injustice sore
And febrile consciousness contemplates
With chilled (and chilling) irrationality
Another's death.
I would hasten from this place
And flee into the warmer folds of night.
    My light is gone—
I soon must die into dark, unknown depths
Beneath this surface darkness.
I seem to sense harsh, grating hissings
Of indrawn breath;
Someone is about to speak.
I fade.
Judge well what you may see.
Judge well
And learn.
    It is dark and cold.
Where shall I find warmth and light?

> *The robed and cowled figure fades;*
> *Light—imperceptible at first—*
> *Illuminates all:*
> *One in garments richly ornamented*
> *With costly threads*
> *And pendant stones of ruby-fires,*
> *Turquoise as the blue of ocean-depths*
> *Immemorial beneath men's sight.*
> *Seated on the highest seat*
> *(Cathedra for the High Priest designated),*
> *Bathed in bloody streams of bloody light,*
> *He bears the crown and name of* **Noah**.
> *Another, seated at the farthest*
> *From the king,*
> *A young man,*
> *Fair of face and form,*
> ***Alma** named,*
> *Coolly framed in irradiating white.*

*And a third, **Abinadi**,*
Stands bound in heavy chains,
His head and shoulders proud-erect.
Behind these three, the faceless mob of Noah's priests,
As silent, hooded statues contemplate the scene.

<u>Noah</u>: This night have we convoked a solemn court
To try, to sentence one who threatens us,
Who threatens you
And all who acquiesce to those decrees
That here are law and right.
As all may see, we arrogate unto ourselves
The High Priest's Throne and might,
More justly to determine by the laws of men
And gods—
In us made one
And thereby unimpeachable for all—
Just execution for his heinous speech and acts.
    Abinadi, a prior warrant stands by which
Your life,
Your limbs,
In forfeiture belong to Crown and State
As consequence of bold seditiousness.

It was reported me	<u>Alma:</u> It was reported me
That you had fled in	That you had fled in
Fear and terror beyond words	Fear and terror
Into the wilderness	Into the wilderness
Lest you be apprehended	Lest you be apprehended
In your madness	In your truth
By my angered folk	By a mindless folk
For speaking	For speaking
As a mindless beast	As an angered Seer,
Bellowing of sin	Castigating sin,
Adultery	Adultery,
Idolatry,	Idolatry,
Unto a people	Unto a people
Rigid in upholding laws	Vacillating in the Law
By custom amplified.	Of God.

It pleases me, Abinadi, to see you
Bound before this throne—the High Priest's Throne—
By me now filled as King and Priest,
For judgment of your deeds.
    Now speak: you next to us in place and power,
Pull back your cowl and address this Throne.
What charges now appended to the first
Stand witness against this maundering old man?

<u>Priest</u>: King and Lord!
As all here know,
This man, Abinadi,

Was found	<u>Alma</u>: Was heard
Inciting riotous upheaval	Proclaiming Truths
In our streets.	Upon our streets.
Attempting to incite, that is,	
Since none were found among our folk	
To listen to the lies.	<u>Alma</u>: To heed the warnings
And low appeal	And true prophesies
Of such a misdirected,	Of a mind inspired to
Febrile mind.	Lucidity.
Our people stood	
In strict obedience	<u>Alma</u>: In lewd obedience
To laws and to our sanctified	To wickedness first
Traditions	Instituted
Established by long centuries	By the greed voluptuous
And by your will—	Of a craven, weakened king.

Thus none were trapped in his ill-formed snares.
The man himself stole in by dusk,
Mantled in the husk of dying day,
Through the Sacred Gates of Gold
From which he had but short time since
An exile fled,
Escaping righteous wrath.
He entered, dressed in ragged filthiness,
With dust besmeared, and mire, as if a herdsman
Sweaten-cloaked, or a farmer's man
Benumbed by ignorance and sloth.

In this disguise he crept among our midst,
Then threw off guile, lewdly to proclaim
His madness to our healthy minds.

Chorus of Priests: Thus he spake:
Woe unto this Folk!   *Alma:* Woe unto this Folk!
Because of black unrighteousness
This people shall be cowed, enslaved,
Hunted and destroyed.
The carrion-eaters—vultures, jackals,
Slavering dogs now crouching in the wilderness—
Shall rend their flesh,
Denude their skeletons of flesh.
     Thus he spake:
Woe unto this Folk!   *Alma:* Woe unto this Folk!
The life of Noah shall be as a fire-scorched cloth,
Tinder-dry and fearful of all flame,
'Til touched by hated fire's bloom;
As a mantle crusted with fine gems and works of gold
In a glowing furnace negligently cast,
He shall erupt in flame,
Swirl in a flood of flames.
No ark may succor him, lift him from
His destined fate—pre-destined by his Will—
Unto the Mountain of all Blessedness,
Save only true repentance, contrite pain.
     Thus he spake:
Woe unto this Folk!   *Alma:* Woe unto this Folk!
The Lord shall visit it in wrath,
With sorrows, famine, pestilence,
Until the sinning eyes of Nephi gush
With burning tears
Until the sinning hearts of Nephi flame
With humble blood;
And from the East a drying wind shall rise
To parch the land;
The dust shall be as insect hordes,
Ravenous, hideous, writhing through hot air,

Ravaging your bounty in their hunger;
And hail shall destroy frail crowns of grain
Which formerly had borne their heads on plain and slope.
    This he spake:
Woe unto this Folk!   *Alma:* Woe unto this Folk!
Whose King and Priests
And all who follow them
As sterile thistle-seed shall toss upon wild winds.
Woe to unrepentant hearts.
    Thus he spake:
Woe....   *Alma:* Woe....

Abinadi: Woe....

Noah: Enough!
These words alone suffice it to condemn,
That witnesses so state vile words
This blasphemer out-breathed.
Do any wish to question the accused
Before his Death-pronouncement is enforced?

                               Alma: Already sentenced
                                         Without hope.

Priest: You claim divine appointment.
Can you explicate a simple passage
From the Sacred Plates?

Abinadi: According as the Lord inspires me
Shall I make answer.

Priest: Say then, what means the prophecy:
            How sweet upon the mountain heights
               Are their feet who Peace announce
                   And gladsome tidings speak,
              Who bear the joys of blessed things,
            Who say 'Rejoice, God reigns supreme!'

Abinadi: Priests, you call yourselves!
Adulterers you are, in blackest veils
Of sin, who seem to teach true doctrines but
Do not! You claim to teach,
Yet great perversions do you teach—
For understanding what this prophecy
Includes, you have denied its deepest truths.
Your hearts are too unwary and too hard
To understand eternal Truths.
What do *you* profess to teach?

Priest: We teach the law of Sinai....

Abinadi: ...And live it not!
You are cursed by God for your perversions
And your lying tongues. For harlotry,
Idolatry, for setting of the Chosen Ones aside
And arrogating rights unto another sealed.
Salvation pre-dictates obedience;
You damn yourselves through disobedience.

Noah: Silence!
You are on trial here, not we!
You are the blasphemer and traitor,
You insolent, seditious fool!

Abinadi: Not I, but you are cast off from the Lord,
To die in beggared terror....

Noah: No more! Bear him hence and whip him unto
Death! There is no cause to prove his guilt:
His words removed the burden from our minds
And clearly stand against him now in treasonous
Intent against this Crown. Only death
Can pacify this madman's tongue.

> *Three sable robes move out toward Abinadi,*
> *Three white hands reach,*

Pallid hands of eager Death,
To lead him to their realm.
No faces seen,
No breath of life—
Shadows merely
Against the night.

<u>Abinadi:</u> Stay! No closer;
Lest the glowing unburnt fires of my calling
Consume you in your sins....
    I must speak!
And as I do, none dare to move,
For if you do, unwanted, frightened death
Shall reach for you—as these to me have reached,
Death's ignorant and servile messengers,
Unaware in what proximity they stand
To final reckonings—and count you as
His own.
    You see in me a power grow, a light
Burst forth as if a flame of crystal sun-white fire;
You have no force to wrest my life without
Consent of Him whose Voice as mouth I stand;
No force to wrest my life, nor contradict,
Nor touch until my calling is complete.
I pray it might touch willing hearts and lead
You back to God. I fear lest—unrepentant—
You me shame, condemn to villain's death;
For what you do to me is Type and Shadow
Of your future state—
If you believe, repent, and follow me,
Life is yours, beyond imagination
Glorious.
    Repent!
    Believe!
And live felicitous.

II

Abinadi: This is my witness and my truth:
The words preserved upon our Sacred Plates
Must surely come to pass. A Savior come,
Redemption's grace extend unto all life.
Belief I cannot force on unwilling hearts,
Nor would were such coercion fruitful in
This life or in the Afterlife that must
And shall overtake us all at length,
Wherein the Truthfulness of things
I here have spoken shall be known—
For all must stand for judgment unto Him
(It boots not whether you believe or not,
Since His existence rests not contingent
On our belief, but self-existent He
Commands our souls).
If you believe, I join in your rejoicings;
If not, I dedicate my life and blood
As twin testators to my dying words.
In death shall I triumphant seal my words.
In death.   *Alma:* In death shall all be lost
                    That he has brought and bought
                 Through suffering incipient and shame
                         Before the eyes of men.
                       A source of light, of truth,
                          Of life for withered souls
                    Parched and wilted in this desert-land
                       Of willfulness and pride and sin.

Noah: Seize this necromantic fool—bind his eyes
That he no more may cast his wily spells
Upon our hearts and bind our hands
With chilling, magical, illusive power.
Bear him out and slay him—
Spare no torture-pains as you instruct
Him of his wrongs; the greater suffering

He feels, the greater expiation for his words.

Alma: May I speak?

Noah: The youngest of our number—youngest both
In years and service to this Monarchy
And to his god—begs his leave to join
His words to ours.
Granted. Speak.

Alma: I almost fear to raise my voice
Before this company of assembled Temple-Lords,
Since youth and inexperience are ill-prepared
To counter wiser, older minds;
Yet force impelling urges me to rise
And plead this man's defense, his life preserved.

Noah: You know our mind, and yet presume to speak
In opposition to your peers.
Nay, to flaunt your ignorance,
Your sentimental, empty ignorance
Before superiors, and counter-speak
Your Lord and King?

Alma: In opposition, no; for moderation,
Yes. For well I know—as you must know
Who sit before the High Priest's gaudy seat—
That much of Truth exists in this man's words.
We of the priestly class are taught
According to the engravings given us
From our Fathers' hands, from Nephi's hands
(Who braved the perils of the raging seas,
Parched deserts and dark wilderness
But to establish justice in this land)—
From Nephi's time, I say, until our own.
And yet I see us daily breaking laws,
Ignoring true morality
For pleasure's evanescent charms.

Can we not learn
From this man's words   *Abinadi:* O learn from my words,
Which seem not mad but....   My son;
      O God, allow his heart to grow
      In wide perception of his need.

Noah: Carefully, young man.
You totter precariously on the faithless edge
Of false belief—
Your rank and station may stand sacrificed,
Years of discipline and study,
Desire for service to your God and King,
Should you lose touch with Truth
And headlong fall.   *Abinadi:* And headlong shall those fall
    Who fail to heed what I have given them.
    O Lord, release their hearts.

Alma: This I know, my king.
And yet I dare no longer hold my words
Pent up as if to stifle them
And sacrifice the wisdom whence they spring.
Since I was set apart as priest,
The broad abyss between what is
And ought to be
Has ever widened—
And yet I could not speak.
But now I cannot stand and see,
      Abinadi: O my soul!
Much less assent, an innocent thus murdered
By those hands that defile our laws,
That seize and rape our virgin blooms,
That finger lovingly fine ornaments
Of beaten gold and all the while ravage
Souls, the highest emblem of humanity....

Noah:
Depart! I will no longer
Countenance such brash and heady insolence.

By my sole right as Monarch in this land
Do I divest you here of powers and of rights,
Of priestly office.
You are no more priest, priest no more.
In memory of your former self alone
Do I preserve your life.
Flee!
Be found no more within the precincts of my lands.
My anger kindles rapidly to flame!

Abinadi: Yes, flee, my son—flee!
Come never to the courts of kings
Where porcine kings and black-robed surrogates
Of priestly power defile their name and calling.
Remember me, remember all my words
And spread them wide upon this earth.
Seek true hands wielding authority
Long hidden though not severed wholly from
This world. In you I live.
Flee!

Alma: Farewell, old man.
I pray for you.   *Abinadi:* I pray for him.
And fear for him.
Noah: You three follow Alma   Noah cannot let him live;
The safety of my kingdom   The safety of his kingdom
And my throne   And his throne
The safety of your rank as priests   To Noah's blinded eyes
Is threatened by this man,   Is threatened by this young man.
The madness running wildly
Through his brain.
Follow Alma closely.
And when it may be safely, secretly fulfilled,
Remove him.
He is a danger to the state and to
The Temple-Courts. The words this wizard speaks
Have altered him, his mind have soured with
Imagined wrongs beyond redemption's pale,

Beyond the ministrations of physicians
Or of exorcists. Kill him now,
While we may.
Haste. *Abinadi:* They shall not kill him.
Their haste is now too slow;
He is escaped from them
Forever.

Noah: And now, old man, you stand convicted
Both by evidence born by these,
The worthy bearers of the Priesthood's might,
And by your own foul mouth.
Sentence may no longer be delayed.
Attempt no further tricks of magic or illusion,
Such as those by which you bring to death's
Abyss, and beyond, into that unknown land,
A son of Nephi, corrupted by your wiles;
Speak now of hopes of righteous mercy.
Do you recant your errors,
That you might earn a swift and peaceful death—
Or is the sentence of this court to be fulfilled
With pain and torment to your aged limbs.
Choose.

Abinadi: I defy your court,
Deny your sentencing,
Reject you as my king—or king at all—
Who kill those urged by truth
Against your viciousness
I shall die:
This I know and long have known.
My choice contains no elements of choice
For me. I depend not on your mercy
For reprieve from pains, but on reprieve
Through hearts through-touched, made repentant by
My words, which alone could make my prophecies
A lie. Yet shall my words live on....
Behold, your murderers slink into this darkening
Room, innocent—though through no fault

Of theirs or yours—of Alma's righteous blood.
You will not find the youth, but he shall thrust
Your kingdom and your crown into the chill-swept flood of night.

<u>Noah:</u> You three, report!

<u>Priests:</u> It was as if young Alma were but air,
Dispelling vapors in the pre-dawn night.
There is no sign of him,
Nor saw the guards his path as he escaped.
He is lost…. <u>Abinadi:</u> He is saved.
Saved!

<u>Noah:</u> And you three also, unless he suffer my
Decree. Go. Seek him everywhere.
Return not without surety that he is dead.
    And now, old man,
Your withered limbs shall feel the warm embrace
Of flames. I shall enjoy your suffering.

<u>Abinadi:</u> Rejoice not in your seeking joy.
Behold!
Your world grows dark!

Slowly, inexorably
A veil of darkness filters through the air
Until Abinadi alone is seen,
Standing firmly
Bearing up forged chains
In proud defiance of the night.

III

Nothing
No one—none visible, that is,
For one stands silently obscured by darkness,
Dressed in robes of darkness.

Voice: Alma!
Alma, my son!

> *A point of light,*
> *A taper borne in shaking hands*
> *By a woman draped in grey.*
> *A flickering ray of yellow light strikes the solid back*
> *Of one who stands unspeaking.*

Voice: Alma, are you there?
I must speak with you.
I bring food, clothing,
Words of love,
Kind words of mother-love,
To comfort you in flight.
Speak to me.
Speak.

Alma:
My mother.

Mother: I come....

Alma: ...No closer.

Mother: I remembered you were wont to hide here
As a child,
Skulking in this ancient passageway,
Cowering in living darkness,
Believing your self invisible
If you would neither move nor speak—
A tiny, quivering animal
Frightened by harsh blows
Which accompany all life.
So are you now.
Come closer, or say that I might come to you.

Alma: That cannot be. I must remain alone,

Seeking safety in the swells of night,
Waves of darkness penetrating through
My body shall hide gross stains from sight.

Mother: Master these your childish thoughts:
Now we must act.
You must face the issue of your foolishness
And strive to bring your life
Again into close harmony with those
Whose words are life and death within these walls.

Alma: Of that there is no hope.

Mother: So I feared....
They say you are bewitched by that old man,
That you have lost discriminatory powers
And waver aimlessly through the swirling night.
I would come to bring you home,
Heal your wounded, frightened mind.
But no, there lie no avenues for us.
You must flee in all due haste,
Lest death may overtake you unprepared.

Alma: You freely speak of ignorance and foolish acts.
What do you know of this?

Mother: That my son is mine no more;
That he must flee;
That he no longer merits rank and name
Of Priest,
No more may offer sacrifice upon
The Altar in the Inner Temple's depths;
That soldiers seek his life
To make him answer with his surging blood
For treason, blasphemy, and actions set
Against true laws of men and gods.

Alma:

You speak of what you do not know.
You parrot empty phrases, hollow words
To echo noisily through this darkest night,
Throughout this land forsaking all high Truth—
You are a well of bitter dust
Choking moisture from an arid, lifeless plain.

Mother: My son!

Alma: You speak of what you do not know, you
And all who listen to the glozing lies
And flattery of Noah's sinuous priests,
Who lift lean-haggard faces to the blue
As Noah's High Priest, leaning bulkily
On his parapet of gold, pronounces
Blasphemous and wicked laws
By men designed to men endow with golden promises....
Promises, not Truth.
You listen to his unctuous speech
And wrestle with each other,
Neighbor felling neighbor,
More quickly to debase yourselves
And give your fifth of grain and goods
To feed the greed and grossness
Of King and Priests....

Mother:
But you....

Alma: Yes, I.
I was a Priest.
I once sat among the robes and crowns,
Leaned against gold-crusted seats
In the Precincts of the Blessed,
Judged self-righteously my fellow-men
According to the edicts spewn
From Noah's poisonous mouth
And forced upon that company

Which should have stood obedient
To God's decrees alone...
No, not forced. Never that.
I too embraced the luxury-loving potentates
Who counterfeited men of God;
And I among them brashly acted
Counter to high knowledge smothered within,
For I knew Truth.
                         Even if there were no sentence,
No warrant on my life, I would flee,
Careen unseeingly into the wilderness,
Embracing now sharp thorns and ripping briars
To my breast if they could but excise
From spirit and from flesh the vile memories
Of what I am and what I once have been.

Mother: My son, my heart weeps
To hear you speak so bitterly.
Surely there was magic—evil magic—
In that old man's eyes, to make you turn
Against your own,
Your nation
And your family,
And see in what we do but fearsome wickedness.
You seem to speak, yet voice and words
Sound not as you, cannot be you—
No son born of my flesh could speak such lies,
Transparent falsehoods congealed in deceiving breath.
The old man is dead, well dead;
Forget his ravings, his maunderings
And the fevered maledictions that brought him
Death, defeat, and flames.
His curse lies on you—reject his words,
Forget him wholly.
Surely there is yet some way to reconcile your thoughts....

Alma: There is no way.
My feet are set upon a hidden path

That I must tread, though I cannot see;
It leads me through this unknown deep
To distant, stable shores.
     My love for you lives yet,
For you as mother, parent,
Fond remembrances from youth.
But hatred blooms in me for what you speak—
For your idolatries,
For your disgrace as wife and mother,
Betraying husband for the ways of Noah's gold,
Betraying son for hopes of still-complacent luxury.
I cannot stay.
I must escape the snare
Of this fell place.

Mother: I cannot deny what you have said.
I would try, but I cannot.
I do enjoy my station,
Regretting never what I have done to bring me there.
And yet I feel within the growing seed
Of shame, humiliation for my acts.
Your words impel me—somehow, I know not clearly
How. I am ashamed. Take these small comforts
From a hand still proud but hopeful now to learn.

Alma: I cannot.
But I accept the promise of your heart,
That as you contemplate these words I speak
You too might grow to understand my vision.
I take nothing of my past
But wander shrouded in an obscure future,
Black and featureless,
Where I—to some—am dead forever,
To others not yet emerged
From death's dried husk into a fuller life.
My way is lonely,
Comfortless perhaps,
But better still than that past I knew.

I know not what my life may be—
Beyond a frequent sense of soothing winds,
Cold (not bitter, but refreshing) on my face,
And soundless hints of joys unspeakable,
And lingering fragrances of dawn-blushed blooms
Dropping honey-laden petals to float
Like kisses on sweet mountain air.
What these may represent, I do not know,
But these I seek as my predicted destiny.
     May you soon walk according to your intimations
Of the truth. Until then, I pray for you.
Live well.

> *The old woman slowly fades,*
> *Leaving Alma alone,*
> *Faceless, formless in the dusk.*

<u>Alma:</u> How could I have said I knew the Truth!
What Truth?
I know UnTruth.
I have lived it,
Seen it,
Feared it.
I feared for the old man, for Abinadi,
Left chained,
Threatened with the scourge of blood-consuming flames.
But still I know not what is right, what Truth.
I only feel that all my life
Until this moment
Has been in vain, that all that I have done
Is wrong,
Weak,
Evil.
     What may I, a cast-off priest—nay,
Not once true Priest, bearer only of
That holy Name but never of the office
Or the power—what may I achieve
In opposition to an edifice of fortune,

Of tradition and of majesty.
I stand alone.

Second Voice: Not alone.
Through my death, I form your life.
Do not despair and make my life and death
But things of minor worth.
Grasp firmly to my witness and my truth
And follow where they lead.

Alma: Is this a vision?
Through the night I see his form,
Silhouette against red-raging flames,
Chained by fettered links,
But never bowed beneath the shame.
Can this sight be true?
This is the Ancient One, the Prophet.

Abinadi: Noah!
King by name, though not by deed—   *Alma:* He speaks,
I cannot name   Though not to me
The name your deeds deserve;   His voice is now directed;
I defy you, though in flames   I weep,
I die,   My soul is rent.
My limbs contract in pain,
And fiery breath consumes these ancient lungs
That I no more may speak, but painfully rasp out
My warning song. No waters now may quench
(Save one alone) this fevered flame, parching
Unto death, and yet I will not counter-speak
My words. My words flow truth, and that you might
Well understand—that it might remain
Impossible for anyone to understand them not—
Have I surrendered to your power,
(For none could touch me, save I gave them leave,
Until my mission were complete);   *Alma:* He defies them
I shall die a martyr's death,   In the moment of his death.
My words in flame-blood formed

Shall stand a witness to their truth
And rest engraved upon the lingering tomb
Of history.
I am guiltless.
My blood be upon your hands   *Alma:* Guiltless he,
My guiltlessness a stain upon your brows,   And I to be.
Overshadowing the splendors of your crown—
No ruby deeper crimson shall attain,
Save only in remembrance of my suffering.

                    Alma: Shall thus the Promised One
                           Also face His persecutors,
                           His innocence condemned?

Voices, in a frenzy of hatred: Blasphemer!
Death to the blasphemer!
May the gods seek vengeance!   *Alma:* Thus they spit
Condemn the traitor!   Upon his name.
To the flames!   May God preserve his memory
To the flames!   Through me
To the flames of Hell!   And through my faithfulness.

Abinadi: Behold! as you do to me,
So shall you perish, you and all your seed;
You shall suffer illness, pestilence,
And want; and as wild, blood-stained beasts
Driven by the blasting winds of death,
You shall be hunted by your enemies,
Implacable, enemies as red as blood
(red as brothers' blood flowing on red earth,
Through the furrows cleft in Adam's time
By Adam's sons); and you will suffer then
As I now suffer in this flood of flames.
       My witness seals your doom!
           My witness seals....

Alma: Darkness once again—and the old man dies,
Leaving me...not quite alone, since now

His words and teachings are my own..,
But isolate from all I loved and understood,
Isolated by a force that should
Progress to unity, not diversity.
Where do I begin? Where go? to bring
Regeneration to my priestly robes,
Exchange their midnight black for purest white
And worthy kneel before the sight of Him
In whose dear Name alone I find my peace,
And find the Truth each moment dawning clearer?
By what right do I raise an anguished voice
To preach repentance, faith, and truth,
Who have known unTruth alone?
     But who comes here, this ancient, white-draped form,
As if a spirit from a guiltless past?

Third Voice: The power is within you, o my son,
To cleanse your robes, your soul, in floods of light,
And lead this twilit, thirsting people once again
Unto a fountain flowing with eternal joys
Where stains are not concealed in darkness' blight
But laved away with tears, that all may stand
As purified before the day.

Alma: Who are you? Where do you come from?
And how know you my deeds and my desires?

Third Voice: My life is long and reaches into former
Times, times of joys and righteousness.
Ere Zeniff's birth, before his time, was I
Ordained High Priest beneath the stable hands
Of one who held pure power in patriarchal
Lines transmitted as the right of legal heirs.
As years grew old, I grew in mind and soul
Until, in Zeniff's reign, the High Priest being old,
And soon to die, I was ordained,
Dedicated to his rights and powers,
Became High Priest to serve this promised land.

But Zeniff's sons loved not the truth of God;
His concubines and paramours,
His greed for gold and finery,
Were inconsistent with the holy aims
Of my high ordination
And my sacerdotal consciousness.
I was thrust aside.
Another named High Priest,
He who sits yet on the Golden Throne
(With sufferance from Noah's jealous, anxious mind)
And preaches falsehoods,
Lies,
Deceit,
Unto a people wasted, starved by sin.

Alma: You?
But you are...you were....

High Priest: They think me dead, and so I am to them.
They teach of doctrines spiritual,
And yet deny realities of realms beyond that one
In which they find themselves in power.
There is no interpenetration, spirit
Into flesh, mortal into immortality,
For those who would deny a life beyond.

Alma: I kneel beneath your gaze.
I lie unworthy.
I have served among the number of those priests
Suborned by him who how has crown and throne.
And were it not for one who stood in chains,
Defiantly refusing claim to right,
Condemning oh so visual wickedness,
I might enjoy still my false and feeble rank,
The name though not the righteousness of priest.

High Priest: This I know.
And yet I also know that you have fled

Abominations set as snares
To turn you from your search for truth.
You have been faithful to your vows,
Rejecting winking gold for service pure
(Instinctive purity, since Truth could not be
Taught), denying wanton smiles, inviting
Smiling wiles, while living purity,
Faithful to ideals of womanhood
And service to one's fellowmen and God.
Your worthiness shines through in all you say
And do. Your ordination I accept,
Sustain, confirm as is my right.
Through you, my son, shall Noah's filthy land
Be cleansed as if by flooding flames,
Destroying wickedness with furious heat,
That only few be saved.
Through you shall those believers meet
And share rich blessings promised them
Who keep commandments and traditions
Handed down from Nephi's time—
My Namesake's time, for so my name is called—
That we might prosper in this land.
      My time is short. This darkness soon shall pass
And you must walk in light while I return
To unmatched glories.
Before my shadowed eyes, strange forms now dance:
The vision of a mountain lake,
A willing prisoner enfolded in
The timeless stones and granite pinnacles
Where birds of undiminished whiteness shine
And cleanse their feathered wings in silvered flows.
I seem to see one larger than the rest,
Circling softly in the evening air,
Protective, ever-watching—
Leading his small flock into high mountain vales,
Following the westward-dying sun
Into a land where daybright never dies,
Where floods of nighttime live transformed to golden noon.

He leads his flock, as birds of prey attempt
To overtake, destroy, stain white wings
With bloody death.
      And there the Vision fades; all I see
Is one whose face and form are yours,
Kneeling in the darkness as I speak.
      This is truth.
My time is short.
I must leave.
Farewell
I pray for you   *Abinadi:* I pray for you.
                                                   Mother: I pray for you.

Alma: If what he sees be true—
And something in my heart proclaims it so—
Abinadi died not without effect,
And in my life indeed his life endures.
                                 They are gone.
The voices,
The old man surrounded by hot flames,
The High Priest cool in unearthly white.
      I stand alone—and not alone.
With me I bear the rights and powers of all times,
Confirmed by true authority.
My past—my base affiliations with Noah and his crew,
My persecutions of repentant souls,
My guilt for acts committed, omitted,
That had led, if brought to life,
To highest joys—This past is dead,
Buried in a flood of anguished tears
From which a pristine future,
White-clothed, unstained years take wing,
Emerge into new-dawning day.
It rests with me to make these visions true.
They are given me,
But that will not accomplish what they bring;
I and those who hear me and believe
Must justify the death of one old man,

The office honored by another;
Repudiate a servile king
Fast-bound in avarice and lust;
Make reparation for a priesthood
Deeply sunk in perjury and fear.
    My witness and my truth awaits
His Witness and the Truths of all Eternity.
With eyes unblinded by unaccustomed light
I walk a path that leads....
Where?
I need not know.
The path exists,
And this suffices me.

Lord, be with me still.

Riverside, California
Malibu, California
Meridian, Idaho
1 June 1975-1978, November 1988, January 2010

PART FIVE

PINNACLES OF STONE:

REFLECTIONS OF AN AZTEC WORLD

PROEM

Silver seagulls shadow fading day,
Steely over Pinnacles of Stone.
To chaste imprisonment I withdraw myself,
My being urge to heights beneath grey skies.

Seagulls splayed—I see, yet they perceive
Me not, know me not, even they
Who violate my flesh, misuse, destroy
Me see yet know—yet see—me not!

Thus I seek my penance in this stone,
This Pinnacle of Stone, gilt ablaze,
Beyond, above unthinking intercourse
Of men with men on blackened, busy streets;

Intercourse unfeeling—love not love—
As streams of headlights/redlights circle me,
Pass over, beneath, upon with raucous cries,
Desperate machinery flinging homeward

Men of stone, of steel, metal-cold,
Unflinching as they engineer my death,
Tractors, trucks, taxis toiling, belching
Foulness rising to my Pinnacle.

Forestall the silent flow of chimney-black
Embracing me with poisonous breath as I
Imperial survey the darkening sounds
The clangorous dark beneath/encroaching spewed.
Breezes breathe nocturnal hopes. I sing
As breezes me caress, endearing wounds.

I sing, yet celebrate but what is me,
My enduring soul-flight would I sing

And search for silent reaches of my shores
Where pounding waves or seagulls only broach
Mild innocence—where pinnacles I soar
Reach pleadingly above my wounded self—

Where selfhood only is, or was, or is
To come—where I, another night breathed by,
Ascend the Spires, urge on my potent force,
Greet in silence hopes of unstained dawn.

Autumn twinges through red-crackling oaks,
Forests dark; along my swelling, gentle
Flesh, harvest-fields reaping spoils
Of former spring's fecundity. Endure!

Mists and almost-frosty breath of morn
Blush in the face of Eastern pungency
Where it caresses horizontal Earth.
And in the Pinnacles of Stone, I stir.
And in the Myth of Possibility I hope.

AZTEC

A splendor of spears
vibrates the dusky plains

obsidian blows shudder
the hexagon of death

muted blood-lust
and captive-tallies stand complete

gods appeasable
and famine surfeited in blood-to-be

Smoking Mirror
Southern Hummingbird
gullets and maws
too long empty

in six directions swirls
the splendor of spears—six armies

chanting homeward
from the Flower Battle

to feed emaciated manifestations
of the god

atop pyramids, and wait pregnantly
for sky-casks to burst.

FILAMENTS OF HUMAN FLESH

Filaments of human flesh
heart flesh hang in rags from the
rusty mouth-center of the Sun Stone
in Tenochtitlan

The Heart of the One World
sacrificed
by white-skinned pagan
conquerors who know not

Huitzilopochtli
Texcatlipoca

The gods feast on warm blood
surfeit on human blood
and grow heavy heavy
stone-heavy and unable to move

while swifter warriors
whose God fed with his blood
invade like maggots and corrupt
bloated corpses

fetid and rank
One feast over and the gods
lie as still as the pyramids of stone
where once they breathed.

QUETZALCOATL

Clouds tumble—
    Cloud-pusher breathes
    Ehecatl, lord of air
    royal quetzal-wind
    serpent whirlwind
    breathing clear the skies
        before Tlaloques,
        gods of rain:

Earth trembles—
    Huemac, he whose hands are strong,
    and Tohil the rumbler
    flint of the thunderbolt
    embedded in earth
    cross of the north, south, east, west
    red-black cross
    painted in the green
    of the center of the world:

Fires flare—
    lightning shakes from his sandals
    lightning from his eyes
    light to shame the sun
    (heart-hungry Huitzilopochtli,
    Lord of the Sun)
    light from the white
    and bearded God.

Air,
Earth,
Fire,
And water—
      white water from the East
      floating cloud-houses from the East
      to come—
      fire and earth
      to come
      cloud-borne from Tlapallan
      in the East.

The White God comes again,
Quetzalcoatl
        Lord of Air
        Lord of Winds
        Lord of the White Clouds

Earth, Air, Fire, and Water—
He will come.

Aztlán: The Place of the Heron*

Grey on blue, omen-bird, the heron
Swoops, caught between earth and skies
Beyond the flat salt marshes of Aztlán.

Grey in morning mists—against a sun
Not quite risen—against a golden eye half-closed,
Grey on blue, the omen-bird, a heron

Cries a cry to echo human pain;
Weary Aztecs begin their march to die
Beyond the flat salt marshes of Aztlán.

A blue gem, set in the valley plain,
Lies Texcuco Lake. Its island pinnacles rise,
Grey on blue. Omen bird, blue heron,

Grey on blue: the facets of Tenochtitlan
Glitter. Its pyramids challenge endless skies
Beyond the flat salt marshes of Aztlán.

The Great Pyramid thrusts, stone on stone,
Wings of stone. And Aztec dreams fly
Grey on blue—omen-born, heron-like,
Beyond the flat salt marshes of Aztlán.

> *Aztlán is the legendary home site of the Aztecs; they deserted it, wandered southward, and finally settled on the islands of Lake Texcuco and founded Tenochtitlán.

THE VISION OF THE AZTECS

At dawn
from his temple
Texcatlipoca spoke—
Huitzilopochtli, high-southern-sun—
condemned

them to
parched wandering,
to centuries of grey
homelessness, sorrow, thirst, and pain
until

his stone
image should rest
atop a pinnacled
island webbed to a swamp-rimed lake—
their home.

HIEROGLYPH

Butterfly words curl
in whispers from silk cocoons—
Painted picture words

THE BURNING
Suggested by a passage in Gary Jennings' *Aztec*

Smoke from Cortez' ships
Rises dark as mourning wings
Against grey-silver. The sun slips
Into night. In clotted rings

Flame-shadowed strangers crouch alone
To face exotic gods. As night
Knits web-work carvings on high stone
Pyramids, the smoke *(light*

Now, tinged with crimson) curls,
Twists into strange faces,
Forms obliquely familiar, swirls
Best suited to the Sacred Places:

Quetzalcoatl, white-edged tear
Of smoke; Texcatlipoca—high
Deities of a dying land. Near
Evening Star, golden embers fly
Heavenward. Perhaps the gods appear
Only when they are about to die.

The Vision of Moctezuma

Moctezuma told the Elders of his vision,
Black obsidian vision bird-borne
As the grey bird flew into the Council Room.

A grey bird—cold-colored as dew in a storm-time
Dawning—fluttering among the vibrant colors
Ornamenting the Elders' shrunken arms;

And on its forehead, a mirror
Of polished obsidian. Among those present,
Moctezuma alone perceived in the mirror

All the Stars of the Universe.
And as he watched
They changed—

And in their places stood strange shining warriors,
Metal-clad, who reached and grasped
And wrenched familiar shapes

Into strangeness. As the stars
Died, screams of pain
Wreathed about the heads of dying gods.

This Moctezuma told his Elders
As he became one with the mirror
Glowing in the forehead of Texcatlipoca's messenger.

CHOICES

Holding his hands out, palm up, and
Shrugging, the prisoner spoke
Through an interpreter
To his new

Captors. "It is no wonder, truly,
That I sit here, content, and
Make no move to
Escape

My fate. I will die—as befits
A warrior taken with honor
At the Flower Battle.
I will

Die with a single, quick thrust
Of obsidian and my throbbing
Heart held high
Will bring

Rain and the Gods' blessings
To my land. I will die and
my spirit soar like
An eagle

Toward the sun. And I and
Others of my destiny
Will become eagles
To lift
My Lord the Sun from his den
Of darkness at the Dawn.

And I will spread light
Upon my

World—If I died here.
But if I listen and
Escape, I will age
and wither

And become earth-bound, each day
Nearer to my destiny in the Soil.
And when I die
The death

Of age, I will simply cease to be.
Like a single blossom
On a blooming tree,
A bloom

But one of multitudes that dies
But one of multitudes,
Unknown, unwept,
Powerless

To rise again. And finally forgotten—
My life will be as if
It had not been.
Do you

Wonder then that I refuse—
Indeed, that I demand
My sacrifice by right."
And with

The Dawn, the young man climbed
The pyramid, stretched himself
Upon the crusted
Stone

Altar—lying with the rising
Sun as if upon his breast—
And willed his spirit
To rise.

EPYLLION

Part I

Kyrie Eleison!

Lord God, protect this Land
when the past returns
and Legends come to life!

Before he came, this Land knew of his imminence;
Earth herself inspired in rhythmic swells
with his propinquity—and *Ce Acatl,*
'Year of Prophesied Return'—
prophesied before the Aztec lords
one hundred years ago.
The bearded, light-fleshed messenger appeared
(descent of messenger divine
to warn unthinking, dull mortality)
one century ago
To trumpet his return—
Ce Acatl!
Year of great return
was in each heart and breath.
Priests and seers and wise men knew,
augurers foretold
and portents flamed
ominous in cloudless skies:
> The White One comes,
> The Fair One soon returns
> unto just Monarchy:
> *Lord God of Air! be merciful!*

Deep fountains of the lakes and seas perceived

his imminence and rose in swells to greet
the white and bearded God of Wind
at his return upon bright air-borne beams
outsent at Dawning from the Morning Star;
lakes rebelled against imprisonment
within mud bounds;
Texcuco openly rebelled,
flaunted latent powers to the sky,
and rose to threaten great Tenochtitlan—
waves of blood-red inundated streets silt-paved.
Tenochtitlan fell victim to swift rape
and ravagement of floods supernal.
Texcuco knew, and strove to rise:

> Let floods recede;
> O Fair One, come in peace
> unto Texcuco's shores;
> *Lord God of Wind! be merciful!*

Was thus full swift the year passed by
when flames arose?
Inexplicable, unquenchable, blossoming
in scarlet petals from grey stems of stone;
bright pungent tips in orange clad,
gold and scarlet surgings to blue skies—
upon the turret-pinnacles of stone
erected in the Holy Place,
erected central in the Place of Prayer
to greet fresh Morning's starry Dawn.
So soon a year was passed
and clouds of midnight shadows hovered still
(dark birds of omen and ill-breeding fear)
above fire-blackened limestone pinnacles:
Temple of the Sun, pyre of flames
ascendant to the Sun,
sacrificial immolation
to Fire's sovereign God—
where living hearts once flamed
and stained
the stony altar-bed with warmth

of throbbing blood,
of coursing blood coagulate—
flames portentous flared—
true flames to light the coming of our God:
> Let flames be quenched;
> O Fair One, come in peace
> unto the templed heights:
> *Lord God of Fire! be merciful!*

Thrice had bearded midnight stars distressed
the jungle skies since flames subsided on
the Temple's staircased parapet;
thrice blazed fires through summer's portent skies
as if fixed stars ignited—self-consumed—
as beacons blazed to mark the path to Earth
from where his heart resides,
the Morning Star—
as eagles skreeing through fixed, jealous stars
to conquer paths whereon their god should tread.
Thrice burned the bearded trails across the vault
to raze all opposition to his will:
> Let stars be cooled;
> O Fair One, come in peace,
> through cloven skies descend:
> *Lord God of Air! be merciful!*

The superstitious say that voices moaned,
that spirit voices wafted on night air
as if a sentient remnant of the dead
would whisper warning words into the night.
The ignorant purport that strange lights burned
above the eastern sea that night, before they came;
that seabirds mewed their anguished cries in vain
and chanted death-lays ripped on still air.
But who can know?
The superstitious hear what is not there;
the ignorant would fear the night-bird's call—
and yet ... they came:
> Let sounds be stilled
> and fearful sights be lost;

> O Fair One, come in peace—
> *Lord God of Air! be merciful!*

At last the sense of imminence increased—
our Imperator summoned wisdom's aid
in vain, Nezhualpilli's wisdom sought
for comfort's warmth. Yet none to him was given:
Moctezuma's overthrow foretold;
treachery from sage Texcuco's heir,
for should the boy-child survive his infancy
he would abet the conquerors,
participate in overthrow
and Tenochtitlan's decay into oblivion,
violent descent into dark midnight caves
of Death's oblivion
through fire and gleaming might.
Thus warned Texcuco the Glorious One of fears
and portent's warning charms—the augur
foretold disaster, dearth, despair:

> Let omens fade:
> O Fair One, come in peace
> unto thy faithful sons—
> *Lord God of Winds! be merciful!*

Before they came, we knew, were warned.
We quailed in fear, unsure. If conquerors,
death decreed; if gods, what hope except
in mercy, justice from their mouths.
May Gods of Earth and Sky preserve this folk,
this remnant of a mighty folk;
May all High Gods be merciful to me
when Legends come to life,
illusions of the past return.
Lord Gods, protect this Land!
Kyrie Eleison!

Part II

Gloria in excelsus Deo.
Et in terra pax hominibus bonae voluntatis.

When he came, grey-shadowed Death, as if
with wide-flung wings to blot warm light
of glistening sun upon the white-frothed blue,
it seemed the wavelets felt his imminence,
the imminence of desolation, loss,
destruction absolute of truth preserved
(vestigial truth) among the native race;
so it seemed, for thrice he wavered,
thrice he almost lost his footing,
nearly tumbled from his fragile craft into
the rolling swells of Carib's watery blue,
as unexpected motions in the deep
him sought to ward from silvered, shining shores.
his hidden face, obscuring all but eyes of midnight
flame, consumed by fires' intensity
of inner hope, conviction, and concern.
    The March from Vera Cruz (interminable
it seemed!) elicited no sounds from him,
so sighs of weariness, no sharp intake
of anxious breath in fear of covert foes
checked only by slight, tenuously drawn
respect and superstitious pagan's fears—
or hopes—that those who came from Eastern seas
    Tenochtitlan in flames, its ruined might,
impressed him not, for he knew that would be;
but now his hidden eyes began to pulse
with inward fires, his burdened breast to beat
with more than measured anxiousness, as he
with fevered thoughts he swept through rubble massed
toward the Pyramid, the Crucifix—
its writhing, tortured Christ awash with blood
and anguished tears—borne stiffly in his hands
    None stopped his somber step, nor hindered him
with cries of victory—or mortal pain—
but fell into awed silence as he passed,
a dark-swathed shadow in a land of death.
None stayed his footsteps on the stony stair,

nor deemed it fit to follow his ascent,
but stood in silent stillness as he climbed
and turned to face the dying western sun.
      With arms outstretched he stood, a silhouette,
a shadowed form against the scarlet sky;
and at his feet, beneath the Crucifix,
beneath the God of Love who died for man,
a broken form adorned in sable-green,
in feathers of the wild Quetzal-bird,
lay twisted in the finery of death;
upon his breast, his dying god,
olden breastplate sanguine in the twilight sun.

Part III

Credo in unum Deum.
Patrem omnipotentem.

Who is the Mighty One?
                              The Mighty One is he who is
                              who is and was omnipotent!

This is the Mighty One:
Hunab Ku,
Teotloquenahuaque,
Tlachihihualcipal Nemoanulhuicahua Tlaltipacque—
This is He, Universal God of All,
Creator of all things,
by whom all things have life—
Lord of Heaven and of Earth
and after all living things, creator of Man.
Who is the Mighty One?
                              The Mighty One is he who is
                              who is and was omnipotent!

He is the Mighty One:
Teotloquenahuaque—
He to whom descendant all things stand,

from whom received Earth's breath
the mansion of the world—
to whom this sacred Pinnacle was raised
of hand-hewn lime, mortised with lime
conjoined with sacrificial blood,
to whom red throbbing hearts I hold aloft.
Who is the Mighty One?

> *The Mighty One is he who is*
> *who is and was omnipotent!*

He is the Mighty One:
Tlachihihualcipal Nemoanulhuicahua Tlaltipacque—
Say now the four ages of the Earth
by him created as a House for Life:
Atonitiuh,
Sun of Water—
first stage of Earth,
destroyed by deluge from the deep,
destroyed as Ocean fountains burst the deep.
Who is the Mighty One?

> *The Mighty One is he who is*
> *who is and was omnipotent!*

He is the Mighty One:
Teotloquenahuaque—
Sun of Earth,
next stage of Earth—
destroyed by roilings in the bowels
by quakes and tremors on the land,
that nearly all perished,
that Quinametintzocuilhicxime no longer were.
Who is the Giant-Slayer, the Mighty One?

> *The Mighty One is he who is*
> *who is and was omnipotent!*

He is the Mighty One:
Tlachihihualcipal Nemoanulhuicahua Tlaltipacque—
and this the Third Age,

Ecatonatiuh,
Sun of Wind—
uprooting all, destroying all
with whirlwinds, tempests of his breath—
he who brought upon the winds the monkey-men.
Who is the Mighty One?

> *The Mighty One is he who is*
> *who is and was omnipotent!*

Who is the Mighty One:
Hunab Ku,
Teotloquenahuaque,
Tlachihihualcipal Nemoanulhuicahua Tlaltipacque!
Now comes the year Ce Acatl,
returning of the gods from silvered heaven,
flying on great wings of white—
Who is the Mighty One?

> *The Mighty One is he who is*
> *who is and was omnipotent!*

Credo in unum Deum.
Filium Dei unigenitum.

Who is the Mighty One?

> *The Mighty One is he who is*
> *who is and was omnipotent!*

This is the Mighty One:
Quetzalcoatl, Feathered-Serpent-Bird:
son of him who is the One,
Captain-General of all high Gods,
Vicegerent son of Teotloquenahuaque,
Vicar-General of all high Gods;
This is he, the Mighty One.

> *The Mighty One who is,*
> *Feathered-Serpent-Bird!*

This is the Mighty One:

Feathered-Serpent-Bird, clothed in green,
Clothed in shimmering green, as in the deeps
dense growth about this high and holy place
glows greenly in the noon-day light;
clothed in green and blackest black of death.
Feathered-Serpent-Bird, he is he.

> *The Mighty One who is,*
> *Feathered-Serpent-Bird!*

This is the Mighty One:
Morning Star, the soul of the East,
wind-flight of the God of Air—
Quetzalcoatl, Feathered-Serpent-Bird,
be with us, swift return
O Fairest One of all, white countenance—
return in star-white heaven-vessels.
The Mighty One, he who is.

> *The Mighty One who is,*
> *Feathered-Serpent-Bird!*

This is the Mighty One:
Morning Star, soul of the Gods,
wind-waft soon again to us—
clothed in flowing robes, unearthly white,
with pulsing crosses red-stained, black,
upon the fibrous cloth.
Quetzalcoatl, hasten Ce Acatl,
I wait upon the teocalli,
knife of pure obsidian unsheathed.
The Mighty One, he is he.

> *The Mighty One who is,*
> *Feathered-Serpent-Bird!*

Credo in Spiritum Sanctum.

Who are the Mighty Ones?

Who is the Mighty One?

The Mighty Ones who are,

The Mighty One is he who serves,
Humming-Bird-Wizard!

This is the Mighty One:
Texcatlipoca,
Smoking-Mirror—
Mighty One of great Texcuco,
to whom we turn our sacrifice
nor close our hearts.
Who is the Mighty One?

The Mighty One is he who serves,
Smoking-Mirror!

Behold the Mighty Ones!
Who are the Mighty Ones?

The Mighty One is he who is
who is and was omnipotent!

The Mighty One who is,
Feathered-Serpent-Bird!

The Mighty One who serves,
Humming-Bird-Wizard,
Smoking Mirror!

Teotloquenahuaque!
Servants of Teotloquenahuaque!

Behold the Mighty Ones!

Part IV

Sanctus,
Dominus Deus Sabaoth!

Wholly in deep darkness it had lain,

Devoid of light, devoid of life;
Long centuries in silent stillness lain,
In blackened, airless void confined;

Flames of midnight-gold encased in stone,
Imprisoned in the lithic ribs of Earth,
Frozen flames crackling through warped rents,
Seamy in untamed monoliths

Heaped in granite pinnacles above
Deep catacombs enfolding Time,
Enfolding ageless Time immeasurable
In never-changing stone embrace;
Wholly in deep darkness it had lain,
Undisturbed as Earth matured,
As flooding tears from cælic fountains flowed
And drowned in monstrous deeps all soils,

Rocks, and pinnacles ... yet dry it lay,
Unexposed through eons to
Erosive nature's wearing, smoothing grip
In undisturbed retreat it lay

Until the wrenchings came, trembling earth,
Twisting, tortured Earth in pain
Contorted, wrapped in stifling darkness' bands—
And its protective sheath destroyed,

That when again the Sun burned hot—three days
To waiting, fearful human minds,
A breath to ageless, almost sentient stones—
One fractured plane reflected light

As if obtruded from long solitude
Into the open face of winds,
The laving hands of rain—o gentle foes—
And slowly grew as stone decayed.

Yet years passed by before again cruel men
Such things admired, coveted;
And safely hidden in the fractured seam
It lay, suffused in aureate glow,

Glinting flecks of golden light obscured,
As Eagles silent soared above,
Wheeled in search of living prey of Death,
To satisfy harsh pangs of life.

> Harsh scrape of feet upon loose granite shards,
> Strong reports of blows, of stone on stone—
> Then night-time journey long and tedious,
> Journey dark unto bright flames—
> Passed through living fire
> Impurities repelled,
> Malleable ore,
> Aureate ore,
> *Gold!*
> *Sanctus!*
> *Dominus Deus Sabaoth!*

Through the fire—beneath the craftsman's hands
(Dark-fleshed hands, dusky red,
Of one who labored near the Pyramids,
The Temples of the Holy Ones),

It took its shape: beaten, burnished gold,
To airy thinness shaped, engraved,
Formed in the likeness of the White-fleshed God,
In honor of the Bearded God.

As Dawn first fingers opalescent skies,
A single figure mounts high steps
Upon the Eastern pyramid-facade;
The Priest ascends stone-templed heights.

Above the steps, the altar-stone is seen,
Scarlet in the glow of Dawn,
Deeper scarlet where bright blood has flowed
Amid the splendors of past days;
He stands beside the place of sacrifice—
Stone knife upraised, plumage black
And emerald green shimmers in the air—
Above the bound, recumbent form

Of one who should be slain, whose blood must burst
All naked confines of the flesh,
Whose heart must throb in rhythm with the gods,
Upraised, before the worshippers.

And as the serpent-knife descends to slay,
Fresh, guiltless beams of new-born say
Reflect upon the Golden Breastplate borne
By him who serves the Serpent-God,

Reflect upon the burning, fiery ore
That long reposed in deepest night,
That—ripped by force from Earth's unsullied flesh—
Adorns the blood-stained flesh of pagan priests,
Awaits the coming of the Holy One,
The Bearded God.

Sanctus,
Dominus Deus Sabaoth!

Part V

Agnus dei, qui tollis peccata mundi,
Miserere nobis,
Miserere nobis!

Noche triste!
Night of Retreat!
Swift-paced runners

                                golden glow torch-shadowed
                                flickerings
                                scarlet fiery thick murky swells
riders flee lake-washed
                    ramps
                                screaming mounts frothing
                                wild-eyed fear incarnate
                                smooth-wave-washed stones
                                        bloody
escaping furious rage
ravaged Tenochtitlan
dead Moctezuma's floating citadel
                                        flecks of flame on inky black

Gold laden!
                                        precious bane to drag them down
fleeing midnight birds of prey—
            no more swirl steely gulls
            above Tenochtitlan
            above stained limestone pinnacles
                black carrion fowl emerge

                                                        nocturnal
                        Western furies—
slipping on slick bloody stones
                    blood of man
                    blood of wounded beast
sinking in Texcuco's miry grip
entombed in golden relics ... and decay!

Estramadura's son! Flee!
look not back upon the past:

Yucatan and Aquilar
                        survivors of the cannibals,
                            fluent Mayan tongues;
Tobasco and Marina,
Malinche

TALES THROUGH TIME, BY MICHAEL R. COLLINGS * 201

                    worth full weight of beaten gold
                    Aztec princess
                    Mayan bred into base servitude
                    salvation of her Conqueror
and news of legendary god's return
                                        Great winged ships
                                        as silver seagulls
                                        resting on cerulean seas
                                        bearing strangers
                                        white Eagle-gods foretold!

Agnus Dei, qui tollis peccata mundi!

Invincible army marching on
invincible Tenochtitlan
                                        beneath the Cross
                                        and Sword
                    steely
trains of incense—copal incense—sent
        with linens
        feathers of the Quetzal-bird iridescent
        emerald black
        and golden handiworks
from great Tenochtitlan unto the coming Gods.
Burning galleons
licking orange-scarlet to deep evening skies
                                        maroon in mourning
                                        flickerings of death
savage ruse—
                    defeating mutineers
                    callow hearts homeward turned
Caravels afloat aflame
        hearts of flame
                thirst for gold
                        thirst for pagan blood
thirst unquenched by briny seas
ceaseless burnings on exotic shores.

Onward to Tenochtitlan!
Sons of Spain as Gods revered
                                  received
The Lord Texcuco rich arrayed
                                  plumes of green and black
                                    crying wildly to the wind
                                    Quetzal-bird in pain
                                borne on purest jeweled gold;
Estramadura lodged in barbaric splendors bright
as God revered.

Agnus dei!

And yet not so—
volleyed stones upon a parapet
                                bloody stones
                                beside a fallen monarchy
                                templed pinnacle
                                of death
Cuitlahuac enthroned
Estramadura in retreat
                                                                rout
                    blood-stained ramps through black
                          Tenochtitlan!

Qui tollis peccata mundi.
Christus, filius Dei.
Christ's mass celebrate
                                descent of God to Earth
and then the march upon Tenochtitlan!
Stone by stone, to Cuautemoc's sovereignty
                stone by stone unto steep pinnacles
                to pagan gods

Retreat
        observe as comrades' hearts
        throb redly on high sacrificial stones
        drums of human skin cry triumphal wails

Attack,
                        defeat,
                                            destroy

Cuautemoc tortured for red-gold—

Across wide plains the Quetzal cries its fears.

The White Ones came—
                gods and sons of gods
                to re-create the reign of peace—
                Quetzalcoatl!
The White Ones came—
                with Death!
Miserere nobis!

Part VI

I had hoped, my heart rejoiced in song—
again—my shores in tender welcoming
awash with crystal waves, wind-worn sands,
curving smooth beneath blue, cloudless skies—
adorned with beauties of rich Earth herself;

I hoped, as he arrived with gracious rule
and sought to mold civility through me—
I wept at his defeat through policies
obscured and greed—*Valladolid's tomb*—
wrenching cries of pain from joyful hopes.

My innocents I weep, who are no more;
ravaged by the fevered fires of plague
(to me unknown, until their unclean tread
contagious me inflamed, my innocents),
destroyed by famine, fear, and gleaming swords

Of Conquerors athirst for burnished, bloody gold—
no reason swayed nor temperance controlled
but maddened with sure surfeity of wealth

they swept my plains with thoughtless cruelty
impelled by frantic, black-cowled shadow-men

Denying truths, abhorring false excess
incrept through centuries of ignorance—
I abhor the viciousness of life-
blood spilled upon high sacrificial mounts,
of hearts warm-ripped from living breasts of men—

Such will I not approve. Yet worse by far
this savage wantonness, destructive flames
consuming culture, heritage, and lore—
my innocents reduced to poverty.
The gods who were not Gods deceived my love.

Hope I sing, the Song of Future Years—
Bright visions from my Pinnacle of Stone,
High above the somnolence of death,
Spiteful sleep of conquest and defeat,
Above thin spiral smoke from dying heights

Of Temple-crowned and sinking Pyramids—
Soothing green encroaches on cold ash,
Hiding, healing scars with virgin growth.
In my Pinnacle I draw sweet breath
And look toward the East for Dawning hopes.

HERITAGE OF HOPE

Few came
then waves—
they wore their paths across a hopeful sea
to lands still bright and fresh
unmarred by past mistakes
unbound by heritage and history
open
ready for the quiet tread of faith.
To North and South they came
        to Edward's ice-bound Arctic winter's breath
        beyond deep greenery enfolding bones
                of lost, forgotten man
        unto the fog-banked Magellanic straits
            between grey cold wind-whipped
            East
            and golden, peaceful West;
along the Eastward fan of continents
they touched,
sought out paths
into cathedral hills
        mountains pillared turreting above
        swift rivers' flows
        the chapel calm of mossy glades
            harboring hushed timid breath
            of furry life;
they touched the soil
and as they went
        sweet nectarines sprang
            where spiny cactus had endured
      and apricots, blushed fragrant peaches bloomed
green waving grain caressed the spring

      and orchards wafted breezy invitations
                                    to the bees
As waves they came
explored
subdued
and in the wildnesses carved homes

fling wide your arms—
receive your heritage of future hopes

                                          Riverside, California
                                          Pomona, California
                                   Thousand Oaks, California
                                                Meridian, Idaho

                                  June 1974-November 1988
                                                  January 2010

INDEX OF TITLES

Abraham's Confession of Faith, 128
An Act of Love, 44
After Thirty Years as a Ward Organist, 119
"And My Father Dwelt in a Tent", 58
…And My Truths Failed, 72
Aztec, 176
Aztlán: The Place of the Heron, 180
Baptism—As Light as Snow, 106
Bearing Testimony, 20
The Burning, 183
Carillon, 122
Celestial, 21
Choices, 185
Christ of Universe, 31
A Christic Century, 25
Creation, 108
Creation: *De Materia*, 24
Dedication, 116
The Dionysian Hierarchy First Notices Moroni and His Friends, 86
Double Quotella, 56
During Sacrament, 46
Epyllion, 188
The Faithful Behold the Risen Christ, 54
Filaments of Human Flesh, 177
The Final Vision, 85
For an Infant, 19
For Thy Sake, 103
The Foundations of the Worlds, 33
Gebet der Einsamkeit, 123

The Golden Chain, 107
The Gospel in the Latter Days, 54
Hands, 43
Heritage of Hope, 206
Hieroglyph, 182
Humility is Hard, 121
In Concert: The Organ, 114
In the Temple, 113
Intimations, 18
Islands—*In Memoriam*, 97
Joseph, 50
Keu, 47
Lines for a Newly Released Bishop, 90
Mission Call, 93
Morn, 52
Moving On—Elegiacs, 99
My Witness and My Truth, 144
Nova, 27
The Ode, 9
On Arnold Friberg's *Mormon Bids Farewell to a Once Great Nation*, 76
On Becoming a High Priest, 91
On the Evening of Her 95th Year, 87
On the Grounds of the Manti Temple, 101
On the Last Day of Her Dying, 104
On the Morning of Christ's Nativity, 7
On the Road to Bountiful, 71
Ordination, 95
The Organist to the Congregation, 120
Parable—3 Nephi 8-11, 62
Patior: The Pulse of Pain, 48
Photographs, 88
Pinnacles of Stone,
Playing "The Lost Chord" at Sacrament Meeting, 118
Prayer for Consuelo, 123
Prelude, 55
Proem, 174
Psalm—2 Nephi 4: 16-35, 59

Quetzalcoatl, 178
Reading "The Faithful Behold the Risen Christ", 70
Revelation, 102
Sacramental Song, 45
Seeds, 42
The Star-Filled Canopy, 26
The Steward, 78
Surrogate: The Organist, 115
Telestial, 23
Terrestrial, 22
That They Might Not in Darkness Cross, 57
To Become a Christ, 29
To Think, 32
Translations from *Prayers of Solitude*, 123
The Vision of Moctezuma, 184
The Vision of the Aztecs, 181
When I Shall Die, O Lord, 124

ABOUT THE AUTHOR

MICHAEL R. COLLINGS is an Emeritus Professor of English at Seaver College, Pepperdine University, where he directed the Creative Writing Program for over two decades. He has published multiple volumes of poetry, novels, short fiction, and scholarly studies of such contemporary writers as Stephen King, Orson Scott Card, Dean R. Koontz, and Piers Anthony. His recent works include *Singer of Lies,* a science-fiction novel; *The Art and Craft of Poetry*; *In the Void: Poems of Science Fiction, Myth and Fantasy, and Horror; In Endless Morn of Light: Moral Freedom in Milton's Universe;* and a Book of Mormon epic, *The Nephiad.* He is now retired and lives in his native state of Idaho.

www.ingramcontent.com/pod-product-compliance
Lightning Source LLC
La Vergne TN
LVHW041616070426
835507LV00008B/282